25 GORGEOUS
Sweaters
for the brand-new knitter

25 GORGEOUS
Sweaters
for the brand-new knitter

Catherine Ham

LARK BOOKS

A Division of Sterling Publishing Co., Inc.

NEW YORK

IN MEMORY OF
My Mother

EDITOR: Dawn Cusick
PHOTO STYLING: Dana Irwin, Kathy Holmes, Susan McBride
DESIGN: Susan McBride
PHOTOGRAPHY: Evan Bracken
ADDITIONAL PHOTOGRAPHY: Sandra Stambaugh
ILLUSTRATIONS: Catherine Ham, Hannes Charen
EDITORIAL ASSISTANCE: Catharine Sutherland, Heather Smith
PRODUCTION ASSISTANCE: Hannes Charen, M.E. Kirby
PROOFREADING: Rita Speltz

Library of Congress Cataloging-in-Publication Data
Ham, Catherine.
      25 gorgeous sweaters for the brand new knitter / Catherine Ham.
      p. cm.
      Includes bibliographical references and index.
      ISBN 1-57990-172-7
      1. Knitting -- Patterns. 2. Sweaters. I. Title: Twenty-five gorgeous sweaters for the brand new knitter. II. Title.

TT825 .H35 2000
746.43'20432--dc21

00-030953

10 9 8 7 6 5 4 3 2 1

Published by Lark Books, a division of
Sterling Publishing Co, Inc.
387 Park Avenue South, New York, N.Y. 10016

© 2000, Lark Books

Distributed in Canada by Sterling Publishing,
c/o Canadian Manda Group, One Atlantic Ave., Suite 105
Toronto, Ontario, Canada M6K 3E7

Distributed in the U.K. by:
Guild of Master Craftsman Publications Ltd.
Castle Place
166 High Street
Lewes
East Sussex
England
BN7 1XU
Tel: (+ 44) 1273 477374
Fax: (+ 44) 1273 478606
Email: pubs@thegmcgroup.com
Web: www.gmcpublications.com

Distributed in Australia by Capricorn Link (Australia) Pty Ltd.,
P.O. Box 6651, Baulkham Hills, Business Centre
NSW 2153, Australia

If you have questions or comments about this book, please contact:
Lark Books
50 College St.
Asheville, NC 28801
(828) 253-0467

Manufactured in Hong Kong by Dai Nippon

ISBN 1-57990-172-7

TABLE *of*

CONTENTS

Introduction

Knitting is a simple process. The basic techniques are easy to learn and it requires very little in the way of equipment. It is so self-contained an activity that one can work quietly in a small space, with a minimum of movement, to create a finished item. Surrounded as we are by the mass-produced, with more and more demands placed upon our time, there is a need to express individuality and reduce stress, which knitting does so well. And have you noticed how often your knitting will start a conversation—even if you'd rather be concentrating on your project?

While I cannot imagine my life now without knitting, I do not actually recall learning to knit, though I know I was taught by my mother who herself learned only after her marriage had taken her to Scotland. Some knitting events I vividly remember: the baby's jacket knitted for my Brownie badge, those oversized sweaters in high school, and that every major exam at university was preceded by urgent visits to the yarn shop so that my study sessions could be punctuated by some very intricate knitting. My interest in knitting really took hold when my daughters were young enough to allow me to make clothing choices for them and I had the greatest fun designing wonderfully different little sweaters.

The patterns presented here are not complicated. The shapes are very simple and the knitting is easy. Whether your taste is classic elegance or wildly flamboyant, it shouldn't be difficult for you to create something you can be proud of. As you look through the patterns, you will notice that many of them provide instructions for variations of the projects. A cardigan pattern may include simple directions for adapting the instructions to make a vest, while another pattern may include instructions and photographs for several different styles of bands or closures. Keep in mind that any pattern from any source can be altered if you desire—you just have to give yourself permission to imagine the possibilities.

Before you select a sweater pattern, take a minute to consider why some of your knitted garments appeal to you more than others. Maybe the hem and wrist bands are too tight, which is often a problem in commercially produced sweaters. Are the sleeves too long? Maybe the armholes are too big. Are you unhappy with the neckline? It could be that you would be more comfortable in a v-neck rather than a crew neckline. Perhaps those purchased sweaters go unworn because a cardigan or jacket would be more useful. Remember: knitting for yourself puts you in full control—from yarn, color, and texture to design, fit, and finishing details. Whatever your choices, I hope you will derive as much pleasure from your knitting as I do from mine.

Enjoy!

SWEATER KNITTING
BASICS

Tools & Supplies

Needles

CIRCULAR NEEDLES? STRAIGHT NEEDLES? METAL, PLASTIC, OR WOOD?
An amazing variety of knitting needles is available and it won't be long before you've built up a large collection of them. Needles come in two basic types—circular and straight—and in a variety of materials. Knitters can get quite passionate when debating the merits of their favorite needles. Should beginners use metal needles? Are plastic ones better? And what about wood (bamboo, ebony, and rosewood are popular)? I use circular needles for both flat and circular knitting. They hold a large number of stitches comfortably, taking the weight off your hands. An added bonus of circular needles is that you can't lose one needle, a particularly useful benefit when traveling. For gauge swatches and to knit small modules for patchwork pieces, I like to use short, double-pointed sock needles as I find them easier to handle.

When buying needles for yourself, remember that there is no single, correct needle type or material. These are personal choices and you will find yourself tending to use one type more than another. Just use what feels most comfortable to you.

☛ **TIP:** Don't be too quick to discard needles you don't like. They can always be used to hold stitches on one piece while you knit another. My needle collection once included quite a few long circular needles which I didn't like the feel of and was never going to use. I ended up cutting them in half and now use them as both stitch holders and straight needles. (To form an end stop, I threaded a wooden bead on each one and held a match to the end to melt the plastic enough to form a knot.)

KNITTING FLAT VS. KNITTING IN THE ROUND
Is it better to knit flat pieces or to knit in the round? Discussion continues among knitters of all skill levels, but this is a matter of choice as well as suitability for the particular project. I use circular knitting—that is knitting the pieces in a tube—at every opportunity. You do not have to turn the work around to knit back and forth, so you just keep knitting continuously, going round and round, which makes the knitting go much more quickly. The incomparable Elizabeth Zimmermann has written extensively on this subject and I recommend that you read her books.

SIZES

Many of the knitting needles we buy are imported, and while some are marked with the US equivalent sizes, many are not. The metric system is used in Europe and obviously problems can arise if you are unsure of your needle size. The same applies to circular needles where the needle length is often given in centimeters. Some needles, particularly double-pointed ones, may have no size marked on them and once they are separated from their packaging you have no means of knowing their exact size. Add to this the fact that many needles still in use are marked in the older Imperial sizes, and you can have real problems. Needle gauges are readily available. They are made with a series of graduated holes marked with the appropriate equivalent sizes, so you just poke your needle through the hole to determine its size.

HELPFUL TOOLS

In addition to yarn and needles, there are a few other basics you'll need to keep in your knitting bag. These include:

- A small pair of scissors or snips
- Tapestry needles for sewing seams (large eyes, blunt tips)
- A good, quality tape measure
- A transparent ruler
- Stitch holders
- Safety pins (useful as markers and to secure dropped stitches)
- Needle gauge
- A well-illustrated basic knitting text

Yarn

TYPES

Yarns are made from animal fibers, plant fibers or are manmade (i.e. chemically manufactured). Animal fibers include wool, mohair, alpaca and angora, while plant fibers include cotton and linen. Natural fibers are often combined with synthetic yarns to create yarns with special characteristics. An acrylic/wool mixture, for example, will have some of the properties of a wool fiber, together with the easy-care qualities of a synthetic.

Yarns are spun in various ways to achieve a particular effect, which gives the knitted fabric a distinctive look. For example, yarn may be very smooth or have loops or nubs twisted with it, resulting in a highly textured surface. A yarn may be very fine or it may be bulky so as to knit up quickly. Novelty yarns have the advantage of not requiring fancy stitches to showcase them. Beautiful fabrics are easily produced by very plain knitting and these yarns are forgiving of uneven gauge, which means the new knitter can let the yarn do all the work.

Knitting yarns are typically sold in balls and skeins and occasionally on cones. The ball bands on commercially produced yarns will give you a great deal of information. They will tell you what the yarn is composed of, and give you an indication of the gauge you can expect to obtain. Suggested needle sizes are usually given, as well as care instructions for the particular yarn. Always buy enough yarn to complete your project as the yarn may not be available in the same dye lot later or may even be completely sold out. Unused balls can usually be returned to the yarn shop or put into your yarn stash for future use.

☛ **TIP:** Chenille yarns are not spun, but are made by wrapping a central core of yarn around groups of cut yarns. The yarn has a velvet look to it but needs to be knit very firmly, so although its luxurious appearance is very tempting, I would not recommend it for beginners.

YARN STASHES

No doubt you've heard people commenting about enthusiastic cooks who have large collections of cooking utensils, umpteen dozen pots and pans, and every cooking gadget ever produced? In fact, my chef friends seem to regard such acquisitions as signs of serious attention being paid by a skilled and interested cook to his or her art. Quite so. And yet, we don't generally find the same attitude being extended to those of us who express ourselves in yarn. Somehow, we manage to feel guilty, that we must use it all up, that we must finish this project before we start another one. I have real difficulty comprehending this attitude; does it prevail because yarns are regarded as raw materials, something you have to DO something with? Do we tell button collectors they must USE their buttons?

Serious knitters generally have more than one project going at a time—some projects are just too intricate to work on unless uninterrupted time is available. We knit for joy, not to turn it into a chore. The days of mass production are well and truly here; we knit for creative self expression. So those of us who are laboring under some misplaced notions of guilt can either get over it or knit ourselves a hair shirt! Come to think of it, even that might be a problem, when you consider that today's yarns have increasingly become little works of art, particularly the wonderfully textured novelty yarns, and the treasures so carefully produced by those dedicated hand spinners and dyers. There is something very appealing about an attractive container of luscious yarn. People who don't know one end of a knitting needle from another will decorate their homes with a beautiful basket of yarn so why should we feel guilty? People joke about the size of their yarn stash, and kid about it being good for insulation and about investing against possible shortages followed by price hikes, but to me the delight to be gained from a lovely ball of yarn is in itself an investment, in my mental health if nothing else. This certainly does not mean, by the way, that such a stash need be an expensive business, for there is a very great difference between buying cheap yarn and buying yarn cheaply. All yarn shops have bargain bins – those odd balls which present great opportunities to acquire bargains.

I like to keep my special yarns visible in containers. They make simple, attractive groupings anywhere in your home (or office!). Just looking at these yarns affords me great pleasure, and inspiration comes so much more readily when I can see what I have to work with.

As you begin to acquire your own stash, do your best to keep it free from little creepy crawly things who would like to snack on it. I make it a habit to put new acquisitions of woolen yarns in the freezer for several days before introducing them to my other yarns—a sort of quarantine period. A regular check on your yarn boxes or cupboards is a good idea to make sure there have been no invaders.

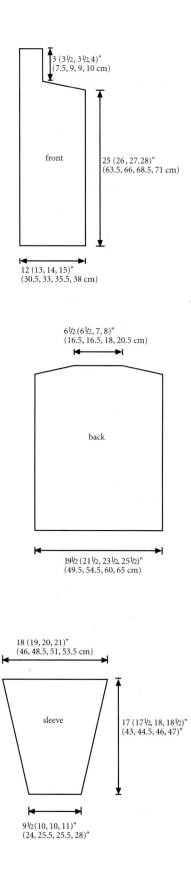

3 (3½, 3½, 4)"
(7.5, 9, 9, 10 cm)

front

25 (26, 27, 28)"
(63.5, 66, 68.5, 71 cm)

12 (13, 14, 15)"
(30.5, 33, 35.5, 38 cm)

6½ (6½, 7, 8)"
(16.5, 16.5, 18, 20.5 cm)

back

19½ (21½, 23½, 25½)"
(49.5, 54.5, 60, 65 cm)

18 (19, 20, 21)"
(46, 48.5, 51, 53.5 cm)

sleeve

17 (17½, 18, 18½)"
(43, 44.5, 46, 47)"

9½ (10, 10, 11)"
(24, 25.5, 25.5, 28)"

Techniques

PATTERNS & SCHEMATICS

So you're ready. You have a pattern suitable for your project, you have yarn, you have needles. At this stage it's a good idea to read through the pattern carefully to familiarize yourself with what you will be doing. Some new knitters feel intimidated by the instructions, but there is no need to be. The pattern is laid out in a series of steps to be followed, starting with a description of sizes and of the materials needed. The designer will have used a particular yarn, but you may substitute a different yarn if you like, provided that you EXACTLY match the gauge.

Pattern instructions are usually given in a range of sizes. Determine which size you are going to use and mark it in some way to highlight your requirements. (If you don't want to mark the pattern itself, photocopy it and then mark it up. Photocopies are also useful so that you don't have to carry the whole pattern around with you.) To determine your size, check the measurements given for the garment. The schematic, which is a diagram of the knitted pieces with the measurements indicated on it, shows the finished measurements. Do remember that even if your bust measurement is 34 inches (86 cm), the finished garment is unlikely to measure 34 inches, unless you are knitting a second skin, because all patterns have ease added to them. This extra width, which often surprises new knitters, provides wearing comfort. Measure your favorite loose-fitting sweater and you will likely find that it actually measures quite a bit more than you are accustomed to thinking of as your "size."

The schematic also gives finished lengths so you can decide in advance if you want to adjust the body or sleeve lengths. It is a good idea to keep a record of any changes you make in case you want to knit this again later, as well as noting for future reference what gauge you achieve in a particular yarn.

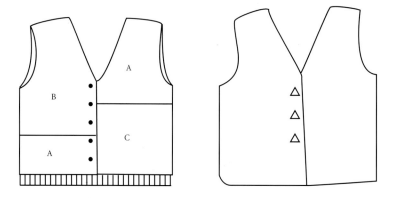

ABBREVIATIONS

Review the abbreviations in your pattern instructions before beginning to make sure that you understand them. If you are unsure about a particular technique, refer to a basic knitting text or ask a knitting buddy to explain it to you.

CASTING ON

There are many ways to cast on. Some have very specific applications, but the general purpose of casting on is to give an appropriate edge to your knitting. Knitters all have their favorite methods, but the two most often used are the cable cast on (which has an attractive cabled edge) and the long-tail cast on. The cable cast on gives a firm edge while the long-tail cast on gives a more elastic one. These two methods should serve you well and a review of them can be found in any basic knitting text.

☛ **TIP:** If you tend to cast on or bind off too tightly, use a needle size one size larger.

BINDING OFF

Similarly, there are various ways to do this but the purpose is the same as casting on—to give a finished edge to the knitting. If you bind off too tightly you will distort the work. I prefer to use a short sock needle for binding off. When binding off in a pattern stitch, such as a rib, alternate the knit and purl stitches as appropriate to keep the knitting elastic.

INCREASING AND DECREASING

At some point in your knitting you will need to increase or decrease stitches. This simply means adding more stitches or getting rid of some. Again, many methods of doing this are available to you, so refer to a basic knitting book or a knitting buddy if you need a review. When increases or decreases are worked at the side of the knitting— that is at the seam edges—make it a habit not to work them on the very first stitch, but rather one or two stitches in from the edge to form a nice, straight edge to the knitting. Straight edges are easier to join neatly in the finishing process.

☛ **TIP:** Working increases/decreases one or two stitches in from the edge gives a nice, straight edge to the knitting, making it much easier to neatly join the pieces together.

Common Abbreviations

*	Repeat from * as many times as indicated
alt	alternate
approx	approximately
beg	begin or beginning
BO	bind off
cm	centimeter(s)
CO	cast on
cont	continued or continuing
dec	decrease or decreasing
g	gram
inc	increase or increasing
K	knit
ktog	knit two sts together
kg	kilogram
m	meter(s)
MC	main color
mm	millimeter(s)
oz	ounces
patt	pattern
P	purl
rem	remain or remaining
RS	right side(s)
ssk	slip 1 stitch as if to knit, slip one stitch as if to knit, then knit these two sts together
st(s)	stitch(es)
St st	stockinette stitch(es)
tog	together
WS	wrong sides
yds	yards
yfd	yarn forward

GAUGE

The importance of obtaining the correct gauge cannot be over emphasized. If your gauge differs from that used in the pattern, your garment will not be the right size. Even a small difference in gauge such as ⅛ inch can make a considerable difference in the finished size of your garment. To measure your gauge you will need to knit a sample piece using the same yarn you will use for the garment. This sample piece, or gauge swatch, should be at least 4 inches square, but preferably larger than this so that you have sufficient knitting to measure accurately.

First cast on enough stitches using the suggested needle size and knit several inches. Then place the swatch down flat to measure it. If you intend to launder your garment, wash the gauge swatch before measuring. Measure in from the edges so that you don't include the first and last stitch of the swatch (edge stitches are easily pulled out of shape and can affect the accuracy of your gauge measurement) and don't stretch the swatch. I like to use a clear plastic ruler (the type used by quilters) so I can use the weight of the ruler to control the piece of knitting. Place pins vertically to indicate where you will start measuring, then count the stitches in exactly 4 inches (10 cm) of knitting, even the fractions. Divide the count by four to get your particular gauge.

☛ **TIP:** Be careful not to stretch your swatch when measuring your gauge and never include the edge stitches, which distort easily, in your measurement.

If your swatch gauge does not match the pattern gauge, you will need to change the size of your needles and make another swatch. How do you know what needle size to change to? If you have more stitches than the pattern calls for, your work is too tight so you'll need a larger needle. If, on the other hand, you have fewer stitches, this indicates that your stitches are too loose and you will need a smaller needle to tighten them up.

Once you've finished a project, your gauge swatch can be put to some fun uses if you like. Hobby supply stores sell blank greeting cards with cutouts especially designed to showcase artwork such as photographs, sketches, and the like. You can use your gauge swatches in these cardboard mounts and display them or use them as greeting cards.

☛ **TIP:** Keep your finished swatch handy as you knit to check against your work.

Finishing

Pay careful attention to the following finishing steps and don't be tempted to rush them in your eagerness to be done. Beautiful finishing will set your work apart.

BLOCKING

Blocking is the process of smoothing out the knitted pieces to the correct size and shape before you assemble them. I usually prefer the wet blocking method: it's simple, safe for all yarns, and always gives me good results. To block a piece of knitting, first pin it out to the correct shape, using blocking pins. The pins are made of stainless steel so they don't rust and are available at any good yarn shop. Position the pins at regular intervals all around the edges of the knitting, then check that the pieces are the right size by comparing them to the schematic.

You will need to work on large, flat surface. Blocking boards designed for this purpose are available, or you can work on the floor with a towel under the knitting. Once your pieces are pinned out, spray them lightly with water and leave the knitting to dry. It's amazing how this improves the look of the knitting.

☛ **TIP:** Treat yourself to a blocking board. They come with a grid-marked pad and can be moved about easily.

PICKING UP STITCHES

Sweater patterns may call for picking up stitches so as to place a finished edge on a knitted piece. Sleeve bands on vests, front edge bands on cardigans and jackets, and neckbands are examples. When you are picking up a large number of stitches, circular needles may be necessary because they come in much longer lengths than straight needles.

Beautifully finished bands are not difficult to achieve if you follow a few simple steps. First divide and mark the edges of the knitting where the stitches will be picked up into equal segments. Count the rows between the markers to ensure even spacing. (Safety pins work well as markers because they won't fall out of the knitting.) With the right side facing you, carefully separate the edge stitches so that you can see the small space (or hole) between each row of knitting. Push the needle through the hole to the back of the work, then place the yarn around the needle as if to knit and draw a loop of yarn through with the needle. Continue along the edge in this way, picking up the stitches at a ratio of two stitches for every three rows. (In other words,

Checking the number of stitches

Too few stitches

Too many stitches

Correct number of stitches

you will miss every third space.) When all the stitches have been picked up, continue knitting the bands in the desired pattern stitch.

Remember that the number of stitches you end up with is dependent on the number of rows in the edge you are picking up from. You may end up with a different number of rows than called for in your instructions if you have changed the length of the piece or if your knitting style or yarn choice changed the gauge.

It is difficult to see whether the stitches have been picked up evenly when they are bunched together on the needle. Unfortunately, some knitters don't check the fit of the garment before completing the finishing. It is very disappointing to find that the neckline fits poorly or that bands don't lie flat, and yet this problem can easily be remedied. Try this method to check the fit: Thread a bodkin with a contrasting color thread and take the stitches carefully off the knitting needle. Adjust them evenly on this thread so you can see how it will look when bound off. If you have too many stitches, your band will be wavy. If there are too few, it will pull in. Count the stitches and decide how many to add or remove. When you are satisfied place the stitches back on the knitting needle and complete the bands.

☛ **TIP:** Don't groan if you have to unravel the knitting to make band adjustments. It takes only a few minutes and is well worth it. After all, if you hate the fit, you won't wear it, will you?

Close-up of knit-in bands

NOTE ON BUTTONS AND BUTTONHOLES

For small buttons (less than ½ inch), an eyelet works well. This is very simply worked. First bring the yarn forward and then knit the next two stitches together. This is generally done on the right side of the knitting.

If you have forgotten to make buttonholes and provided you can use a small button, you can add them by carefully separating the stitches at the appropriate place in the button band and working a buttonhole stitch around the buttonhole you have just made.

☛ **TIP:** Don't make buttonholes any larger than they need to be— knit fabric is very elastic. If a buttonhole turns out too big or later stretches, you can easily stitch it smaller.

SEAMING

This is a simple process, even for those who don't sew. In most cases the work is sewn up with the same yarn used to knit it. If the yarn is highly textured, though, it may be difficult to pull easily through the knitting or it may break. In these cases, choose a smooth, matching yarn for sewing up your work. Needlepoint yarns and embroidery flosses, which are available in a vast array of colors, are ideal, as you can separate the strands to get the right thickness of yarn. Choose threads whose cleaning requirements will be compatible with the yarns used in the garment. Don't, for example, sew up a cotton garment with a woolen thread.

You will need a bodkin or tapestry needle for seaming. These needles have a large eye, making them easy to thread, and their blunt points slide easily through the work. Where pins are needed, knitter's pins are best: their long length and large head prevent them from disappearing into the knitting.

Mattress stitch is an excellent, all-purpose seaming stitch, resulting in an invisible seam. It is always worked with the right side of the fabric facing you, making it very easy to match stripes. To sew a seam in mattress stitch, first place the two pieces of knitting to be joined on a flat surface. Thread the needle and work upward one stitch in from the edge, passing the needle under the bar between the first and second rows on one side of the knitting and then moving to the corresponding rows on the other side. Pick up two bars and return to the first piece, going into the knitting at the same point you came out, and pick up two bars. Repeat these steps, working from side to side and pulling the seam closed as you go, taking care not to pull so tightly that you cause puckers. Your goal is a flat, neat seam.

When seaming reverse stockinette pieces, use the same method but take only one bar at a time for better seam control.

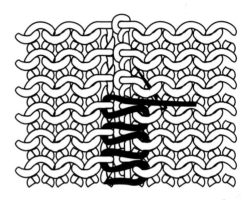

Reverse Stockinette stitch

CARE OF THE FINISHED GARMENT

Always store your knitwear folded, never hanging. Also avoid sealing them in plastic bags; if you must use plastic, leave the bag open so the fibers can breathe. (I use pillow cases for this purpose.)

I handwash all of my knitting, and there really is no big mystery here. What ruins knitting is excessive handling and sudden temperature changes in the wash and rinse water. In other words, don't wash your beautiful knitting in luke warm water and then plunge it into cold water for rinsing; the shock will cause wool yarn to shrink up in horror. Handle the washing process quickly (i.e., don't leave woolens to soak for any length of time), and support the weight of the wet knitting to prevent stretching and loss of shape. A pillowcase or mesh laundry bag is ideal for this and you can then spin it in your washing machine to remove excess water. I also like to add a little hair conditioner to the final rinse water. Dry your sweater flat on a towel.

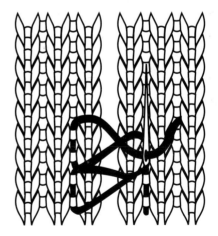

Stockinette stitch

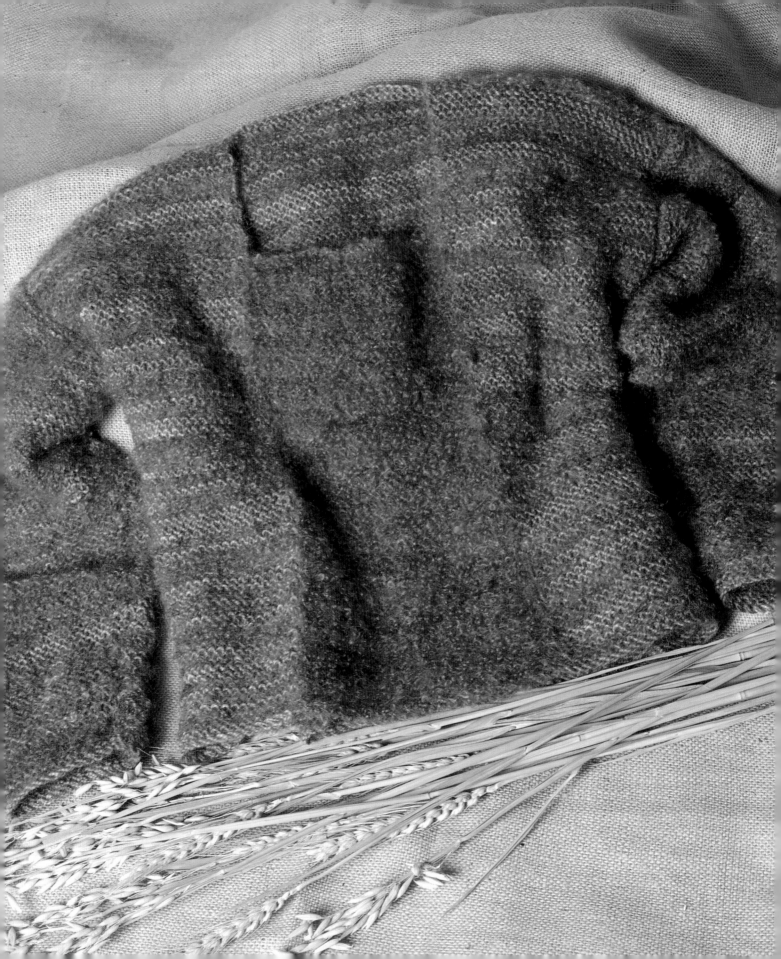

A Simple
First Sweater

After reviewing some of the fundamentals of knitting on pages 12-22, it may be helpful to apply a little of this information to the knitting of an actual sweater. The sweater shown here is designed in a very simple shape, with the body formed by four rectangles. All of the pieces are knit in garter stitch which lies flat and gives the knitting a finished edge. Feel free to vary the design by knitting the panels in different colors or types of yarn. You may also choose to make a design feature of the seams by embellishing them with buttons, beads, or embroidery. Be sure to read through the instructions and study the illustrations before beginning.

MATERIALS
In order to get started we need to find suitable yarn for the project. You are not, of course, bound in any way to use the yarn I have chosen, and the directions that follow should enable you to knit your sweater in any size and any yarn. Joslyn's Fiber Farm has several different qualities of yarn to choose from, and all are available in a number of wonderful hand-dyed colorways. Three of the yarns in particular proved to be very suitable for this project as each knits to the same gauge and therefore affords the opportunity to vary the look of the knitted fabric while maintaining the same stitch gauge. The color and texture variations of the yarn do the work, allowing you to achieve a pleasing result with little fuss. I decided to use two of the yarns: Bubbles, which is a poodle loop and Mohair Myst which is a smooth yarn with a lovely soft hand. The colorway shown here is Heather Morn and my sweater required a total of 15 ounces of Mohair Myst and Bubbles.

GAUGE
The first thing we need to do is make a gauge swatch. Cast on at least 20 stitches (preferably more) on needles of appropriate size for the yarn you have chosen. The ball band on your yarn will give you information on the suggested needle size. Knit in garter stitch in whichever yarn you choose for at least 3 or 4 inches (7.5 or 10 cm). If the work feels too tight, try larger needles; if it is too loose, change to smaller needles.

Schematics for Basic Sweater

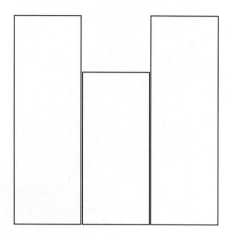

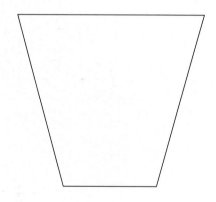

I made a number of gauge samples, trying out different combinations of the yarns until I decided which needle size suited me best. When you are satisfied with your samples, select the one you will be working from and measure it carefully without stretching to determine the number of stitches you get to the inch. This is your own personal gauge, and your pieces will be worked according to it for this sweater. My sample resulted in a gauge of 4 stitches per inch (2.5 cm).

SWEATER BACK

The next step is to determine the size of your sweater. Select a well-fitting sweater from your closet and lay it down carefully on a flat surface. Measure it across the back from side seam to side seam at a point below the armholes. As this is a drop-shouldered style there will be no armhole shaping and the back will be knit as a rectangle (see schematic). To determine the number of stitches to cast on for the back, multiply your inch (or cm) measurement by the number of stitches per inch in your gauge—that is, the back measurement multiplied by the stitch gauge. (In my case, the back measurement was 20 inches, so 20 times 4 = 80 stitches.) Cast on your total number of stitches, taking care not to do it too tightly. Note: No seam stitches need to be added as you will sew all the pieces up using an edge-to-edge flat seam.

Work in garter stitch until you have the desired length for your back piece. (The back of my sweater measures 20 inches in width by 19 inches in length.) Bind off the stitches loosely.

SWEATER FRONT

To determine the sizes of the front panels, find and mark the middle point of your sweater's back. Measure and mark 3½ inches (9 cm) on either side of the middle mark for a total back neck measurement of 7 inches (18 cm). Your back neck measurement may be greater than this, but probably not smaller.

The front will be knit in three pieces: two side panels, each of the same width, and of the same length as the back, and a single center panel which will be shorter in length to allow for the head opening. This center front panel will measure 7 inches (18 cm) in width so it will match the back neck width.

Subtract 7 inches from the front width (the same width as your back) and divide the answer in half to find the width measurement for your two outer front panels. (In my case, I subtracted 7 from 20 to get 13 and then divided 13 in half to get outer front panel widths of 6½ inches.)

Determine the number of stitches to cast on for the outer front panels by multiplying the number of inches by your gauge number. For the center front panel, multiply 7 inches times your gauge number. (Example: In my sweater, I multiplied 7 inches times 4 for a total of 28 stitches.)

Knit the two outer center panels first, working them as you did for the back and in the same length. The center panel will be shorter to allow for your head and in the sample shown here was knitted 5 inches (12.5 cm) shorter. Make the opening larger if you like by knitting the piece shorter. Likewise, if you want a higher front neckline, knit the piece a little longer, leaving a portion of the seam open if necessary. (This gives you an opportunity to use a nice button, fastened with a loop.) Remember, the easy way to make sure your pieces are the same length is to count the number of ridges. Use the tip of a tapestry needle to count between the ridges.

Back

SLEEVES

The sweater is really taking shape now and all you have left is the sleeves. First decide how wide you want the bottom of the sleeve to be. It shouldn't be less than 8 inches (20 cm) in width, but wider is fine. Refer to your well-fitting sweater as a guide. The sleeve increases to 20 inches (50 cm) across at the top, but again remember that yours may be wider than this.

To determine how many stitches you need to cast on, multiply your bottom sleeve width number by your gauge. Your answer is the number of stitches you need to cast on. (Example: For my sweater I chose a bottom sleeve measurement of 9½ inches. I multiplied this number by 4 for a total of 38 stitches.)

Front

Because there's a difference between what the top and the bottom of the sleeve measure (see schematic for basic shape), you will need to increase the number of stitches as you work. The top of your sleeve will measure 20 inches (or 80 stitches), while the bottom of your sleeve is probably about half of that. To determine the number of stitches that need to be increased and how often to increase them, subtract your total number of cast-on stitches for the sleeve bottom from 80 stitches. (Example: For my sweater, I subtracted 38 from 80 for a total of 42 stitches that need to be increased.) Since sleeve increases are worked in pairs—one stitch at each side of the sleeve— you will need to divide your number of stitches to be increased in half. (Example: My sleeve needed a total of 42 increased stitches. Dividing that number in half gives me 21 increases in total.) Increases also must be spread out evenly over the length of the sleeve, so work your increases every 6 rows (that is, every three garter stitch ridges) until you have the required number of stitches. Remember to work the increases one stitch in from the edge to give a smooth line to your knitted piece.

Sleeve

Cast on your stitches and knit your sleeve, increasing at the end of the 6th and every following 6th row until you have your required number of stitches. (In my case, I increased for a total of 21 times until there were 80 stitches on the needle.) You may change yarns as you work or use a single type of yarn. Continue knitting until the sleeve is the desired length. How long should this be? Refer to the sweater you took your body measurement from and measure along the sleeve seam. Remember that on a drop-shoulder style such as this, the sleeve length is affected by the width of the garment and at what point along the arm the shoulder seam actually falls. When you are satisfied with the finished length, bind off your sleeve loosely.

FINISHING

The finishing steps are every bit as important as the actual knitting. Poor finishing can ruin a garment, so take the time to do this properly. First smooth out your garment pieces and check them carefully. Darn in any loose ends and check that there are no dropped stitches.

Stitch the three front panels together, then stitch the front and back together at the shoulder seams. (Refer to the basic instructions on pages 20 and 21 if desired.) I find it more comfortable to work at a table when seaming pieces like these. Place the work on the table with the right side facing you. Thread a tapestry needle or bodkin with a long piece of smooth yarn and work from the bottom of the piece upward. Insert the needle through the knob at the end of the first row of knitting and then insert the needle through the knob on the opposite side. Stitch in this manner from the first piece to the second piece, back and forth, moving up to the next knob each time. When finished, you should have a neat, flat seam.

Measure the bound-off edge of the sleeve, divide this measurement by two, and then measure and mark this amount down from the top of the shoulder. This is where you will sew the sleeve onto the sweater body. (Example: In my sweater, the bound-off edge of my sleeve measured 20 inches so I divided 20 in half and then measured 10 inches down from the top of the shoulder.)

Mark the middle point of your sleeve at the top and place this at the shoulder seam. Pin the top of the sleeve into place between the markers, then sew the sleeve into the armhole.

Stitch the side seams. Stitch the sleeve seams. When possible I prefer to sew from the underarm to the wrist and then from the underarm to the hem edge. (Sewing from the bottom up often results in a slight pulling up of the seam.)

And there it is, your very own design. Enjoy!

CARDIGANS & JACKETS

The designs in this chapter are not difficult to knit and feature some interesting finishing details. Select a stunning yarn for a cardigan or jacket to take you through every season and occasion. Pattern variations are presented, showing you how to make a vest from a cardigan pattern or how to lengthen a short jacket into a coat.

Shawl Collar Jacket

This easy-fit jacket will take you almost anywhere and can be worn over almost anything. Wear it loose or fastened with a stunning pin. I like to wear jackets like this either open or just lightly clasped with an eye-catching pin.

SIZES

Small (medium, large, extra large)

Finished Measurements

Chest: 39 (43, 45, 49) inches (99, 109, 114.5, 124.5 cm)

MATERIALS

13 (14, 15, 16) balls of Plymouth Yarn Company's Adriafil Kermesse (50 g = approximately 58 m)

Knitting needles in size 10½ (size 6.5 mm) or size needed to obtain correct gauge.

Small amount of a smooth yarn in a matching color for seams

GAUGE

11 sts = 4 inches (10 cm)

2.75 sts = 1 inch (2.5 cm)

BACK

Cast on 54 (60, 66, 70) sts.

Working in garter stitch (knit every row) work until the back = 25 (26, 27, 28) inches (63.5, 66, 68.5, 71 cm) in length.

SHAPE SHOULDERS:

BO 6 (7, 7, 8) sts at beg of next 2 rows. BO 6 (7, 8, 8) sts at beg of next 4 rows. BO rem 18 (18, 20, 22) back neck sts. Measure 9 (9½, 10, 10½) inches (23, 24, 25.5, 27 cm) down from the beg of shoulder shaping and place markers for the underarm.

LEFT FRONT

Cast on 33 (36, 39, 42) sts and knit until piece measures the same as back to start of shoulder shaping.

Work left shoulder shaping as for back.

Continue working on the remaining 15 (15, 16, 18) sts for collar for a further 3 (3½, 3½, 4) inches (7.5, 9, 9, 10 cm).

BO.

RIGHT FRONT

Work same as left front, reversing all shaping.

Place markers as on back for underarm.

SLEEVES

Cast on 26 (28, 28, 30) sts.

Increase 1 st at each end every 4 rows until there are 50 (52, 56, 60) sts.

Work straight until sleeve measures 17 (17½, 18, 18½) inches (43, 44.5, 46, 47 cm).

☞ **TIP:** At this point I like to place all the stitches on a long thread until I am seaming the jacket together so that it's easy to adjust the finished sleeve length.

Cuffed-Sleeve Variation

Cast on 30 (32, 32, 34) sts and work 1 inch (2.5 cm) in garter stitch.

Decrease 1 st at each end of the next row.

Continue working until sleeve measures 2½ inches (6.5 cm) and decrease 1 st at each end of the next row. You will now have 26 (28, 28, 30) sts.

When the sleeve measures 3 inches (7.5 cm) place markers.

Increase 1 st at each end of the next row and continue working the sleeves as given for the jacket.

To finish, seam the first 3 inches (7.5 cm) of the sleeve, remembering that the wrong side of the sleeve will show on the right side when the cuff is turned back. Complete the rest of the sleeve seam.

Close-up view of shawl collar

FINISHING

Use a smooth yarn in a matching color for the seams.

Stitch shoulder seams firmly together.

Join ends of shawl collar neatly, remembering that the wrong side of the collar will be on the right side of the jacket.

Stitch the collar to the back neck edge.

Measure the midpoint of the sleeve and place at shoulder seam.

Pin sleeve into place between the markers and make any necessary adjustment to sleeve length here, then cast off sts loosely.

Seam sleeve into place.

Join sleeve and side seams neatly.

Snuggle into your shawl collar and sally forth!

Coat Variation

The length of the jacket can easily be extended to become a casual coat. You will need an extra 5 (5, 6, 6) balls of yarn to lengthen the jacket by 15 inches (38 cm). You can fasten the coat with a pin or add bands and buttons or just wear it edge-to-edge. You also have the option of making side vents. To form the vents, simply leave the side edges unseamed for the last 8 to 10 inches (20.5 to 25.5 cm). Add a decorative button to make a feature of these vents and secure the seam.

Yet another option is to add a central back vent for a more tailored look. To add the back vent you will need to work the back of the coat in two sections for the depth of the vent. Follow the instructions below.

BACK

For the first part, cast on 33 (36, 39, 41) sts and work in garter stitch until the piece is 8 inches (20.5 cm) long.

Next row, BO 6 sts.

Put this piece aside for the moment.

Cast on 27 (30, 33, 35) sts for the second piece.

Knit until this piece matches the first section in length by counting your garter stitch ridges to be sure.

Close-up view of back vent for coat option

JOINING ROW

Knit to the end of the row, then knit across 27 (30, 33, 35) sts on the other needle, placing the 6 cast-off sts behind the work.

Continue knitting on these 54 (60, 66, 70) sts as given for the jacket back, beginning the shoulder shaping when the piece is 40 (41, 42, 43) inches (101.5, 104, 107, 109 cm) in length.

FRONTS

Work as given for the jacket but knit the pieces to match the length of the coat back.

SLEEVES

Work as for jacket.

FINISHING

To finish the center back vent, slipstitch the cast-off sts of the underlay to the wrong side of the back.

Sew a flat button through both thicknesses to secure the vent.

Schematics for Shawl Collar Jacket

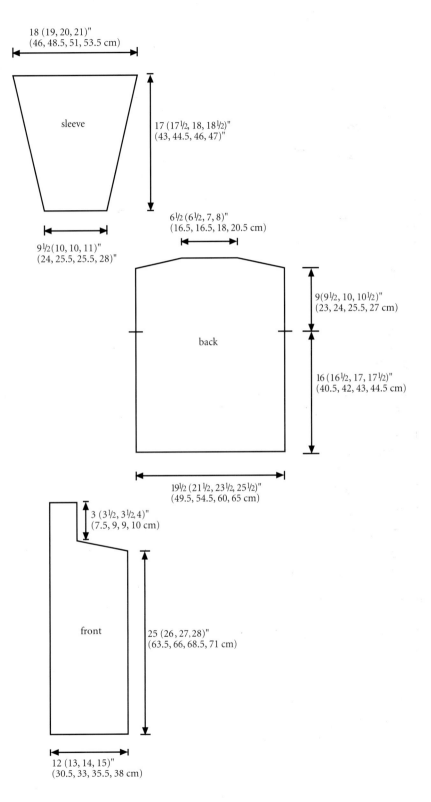

18 (19, 20, 21)"
(46, 48.5, 51, 53.5 cm)

17 (17½, 18, 18½)"
(43, 44.5, 46, 47)"

sleeve

9½ (10, 10, 11)"
(24, 25.5, 25.5, 28)"

6½ (6½, 7, 8)"
(16.5, 16.5, 18, 20.5 cm)

9 (9½, 10, 10½)"
(23, 24, 25.5, 27 cm)

back

16 (16½, 17, 17½)"
(40.5, 42, 43, 44.5 cm)

19½ (21½, 23½, 25½)"
(49.5, 54.5, 60, 65 cm)

3 (3½, 3½, 4)"
(7.5, 9, 9, 10 cm)

front

25 (26, 27, 28)"
(63.5, 66, 68.5, 71 cm)

12 (13, 14, 15)"
(30.5, 33, 35.5, 38 cm)

Finishing Variations

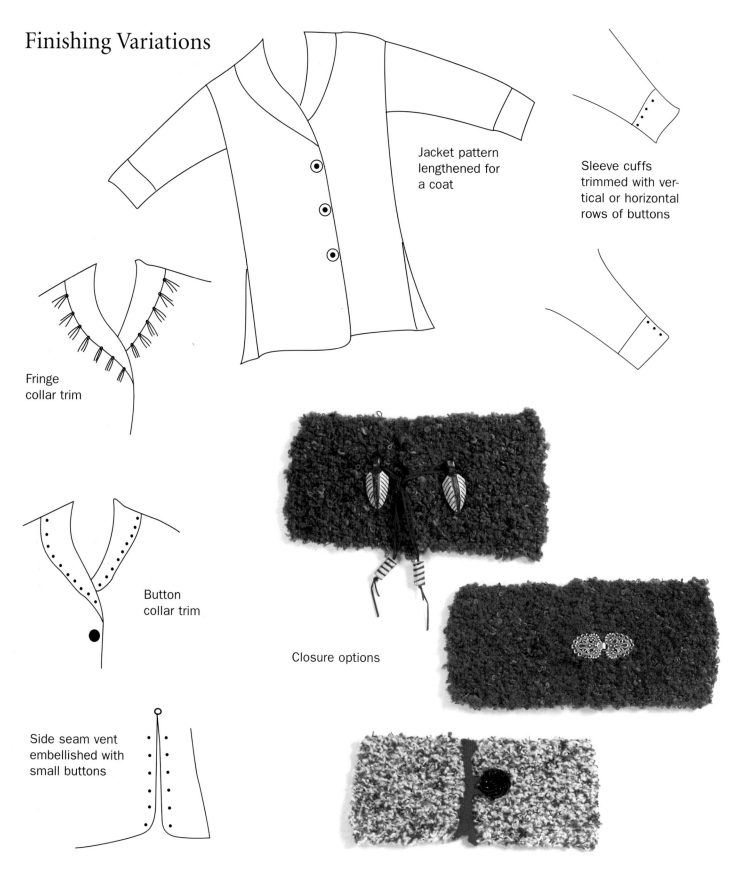

Jacket pattern lengthened for a coat

Sleeve cuffs trimmed with vertical or horizontal rows of buttons

Fringe collar trim

Button collar trim

Closure options

Side seam vent embellished with small buttons

Cozy Cardigan

This super-easy, oversized softie knits up quickly and is just the piece for weekend relaxing. The pattern can easily be adapted to a vest (see sidebar on page 39), and the patch pockets add a decorative touch which you can customize in any number of creative ways.

SIZES
Petite (small, medium, large, extra large)

Finished Measurements

Chest: 42 (44, 46, 48, 50) inches (107, 112, 117, 122, 127 cm)

MATERIALS
13 (14, 15, 16, 17) balls of Plymouth Yarn Company's Dakota
   (50 g = 80 m)

Knitting needles in size 8 and 10 (5 and 6 mm) or size needed to give
   correct gauge

24- or 29-inch (61 or 74 cm) circular knitting needle in size 8 (5 mm)

5 buttons

GAUGE
12 sts and 19 rows = 4 inches (10 cm) over St st on larger needles

This pattern also gives you the option of knitting the front bands vertically. When done this way, the extra stitches needed for the button and buttonhole bands are cast on as part of the garment fronts. When the ribbing for the welt, or lower band, is complete, the extra stitches are left on a safety pin while the rest of the garment is finished. The yarn is rejoined to those stitches and the front bands are worked and then stitched to the garment. The choice is yours. If you choose to knit the bands this way, make sure you stretch them slightly as you attach them to the body of the garment and that they lie flat.

BACK
Using smaller needles, cast on 64 (66, 70, 72, 76) sts and work in K1P1 rib for 1½ to 2 inches (4 to 5 cm).

Change to larger needles and work in St st until back measures 22 (23, 24, 25, 26) inches. (56, 58.5, 61, 63.5, 66 cm).

BO all sts.

Measure 9 (9½, 9½, 10, 10½) inches (23, 24, 25.5, 27 cm) from top of shoulders and place markers for underarm.

LEFT FRONT
With smaller needles, cast on 32 (33, 35, 36, 38) sts and work in K1P1 rib same as for back.

Change to larger needles and work in St st until work is same length as back to underarm markers.

Begin neck shaping: Decrease 1 st at neck edge every 4 rows until 22 (23, 25, 25, 27) rem.

Work until piece is the same length as back to shoulders.

BO all sts.

RIGHT FRONT
As for left front, reversing all shaping.

SLEEVES
With smaller needles, cast on 26 (26, 28, 28, 28) sts and work in K1P1 rib for 2½ inches. (6.5 cm).

Change to larger needles and St st and work increases as follows: Inc 1 st on each side every 4 rows until there are 54 (58, 58, 60, 64) sts on needle. Knit until sleeve measures 17 (17½, 17½, 18, 18) inches (43, 44.5, 44.5, 46, 46 cm) from beg.

BO all sts.

POCKETS
Using larger needles, cast on 25 sts and work in St st, knitting the first and last two sts of every row to form the pocket's neat side edge.

Work until the pocket is about 7

inches (18 cm) long. Change to smaller needles and work an inch (2.5 cm) in K1P1 rib, maintaining the edge sts in garter st.

BO all the sts.

If you intend to embellish the pockets with buttons, sew these on now before pinning the pockets into place on the garment fronts.

Stitch carefully along the sides of the pocket to attach (a firm back stitch between the first and second sts of the garter st border works well here) and slipstitch the cast-on edge of the pocket to the fronts.

Tiny buttons may be used to give support to the top corners of the pocket and can also add a decorative element.

☞ **TIP:** If you tend to stuff your pockets and feel they may "bag out" too easily, try knitting them on a needle 1 size smaller than that used for the body of the garment.

FINISHING

Join shoulder seams.

Mark the button positions along left front with the first one ½ inch (1.5 cm) above cast on edge and last ½ inch below start of neck shaping.

Using circular needle, with right side facing, begin at lower right front edge and pick up and knit sts along the right front; then pick up and knit 20 (20, 20, 22, 22) sts across the back neck and an equal number of sts down the left front as for the right. (Review technique on pages 19 and 20 if desired.)

Work buttonholes in your preferred method when band is about ½ inch wide, positioning them to correspond with the placement of the buttons.

Continue in rib until band is about 1½ inches (4 cm).

BO in rib.

Place the middle point of the sleeve at the shoulder seam and sew the sleeve top into place between markers.

Sew up the side and sleeve seams.

Sew on the buttons to correspond with buttonholes.

BAND VARIATION

If you prefer to knit the bands vertically, add an extra 6 sts to the number of sts you will cast on for the fronts to form the button and buttonhole bands, then proceed as follows.

LEFT FRONT

With smaller needles, cast on 38 (39, 41, 42, 44) sts and work in rib same as for back. Change to larger needles. With right sides facing, knit to the last 6 sts and place them on a safety pin. Continue working the rest of the left front, following the instructions already given.

Join yarn to the sts on the safety pin and cast on a stitch to be used in the seam.

Using the smaller needles, continue to work in ribbing until the band, slightly stretched, fits up to the middle of the back neck.

Pocket Embellishment

Pockets can be embellished in any number of creative ways.

Here are a few suggestions.

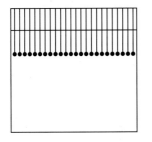

Decorative button attached with leather

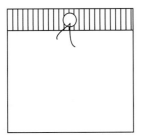

Beaded tassels of yarn or cording

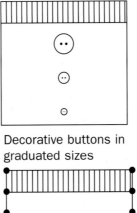

Decorative buttons in graduated sizes

Vertical rows of tiny buttons

Schematics for Cozy Cardigan

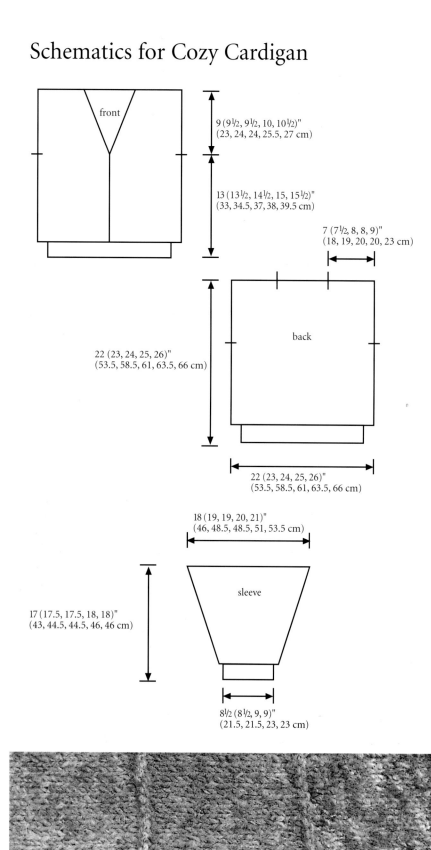

front

9 (9½, 9½, 10, 10½)"
(23, 24, 24, 25.5, 27 cm)

13 (13½, 14½, 15, 15½)"
(33, 34.5, 37, 38, 39.5 cm)

7 (7½, 8, 8, 9)"
(18, 19, 20, 20, 23 cm)

back

22 (23, 24, 25, 26)"
(53.5, 58.5, 61, 63.5, 66 cm)

22 (23, 24, 25, 26)"
(53.5, 58.5, 61, 63.5, 66 cm)

18 (19, 19, 20, 21)"
(46, 48.5, 48.5, 51, 53.5 cm)

sleeve

17 (17.5, 17.5, 18, 18)"
(43, 44.5, 44.5, 46, 46 cm)

8½ (8½, 9, 9)"
(21.5, 21.5, 23, 23 cm)

Thread a tapestry needle with a length of yarn and sew the band to the front, making sure that it lies flat.

Adjust the length of ribbing to end at the center back neck and leave the sts on a safety pin. Mark button placement so that the first button is ½ inch from the cast-on edge and the last button 1/2 inch from the beginning of the neck shaping.

RIGHT FRONT

Cast on 38 (39, 41, 42, 44) sts and work ½ inch in rib.

With the right side of the work facing, work first buttonhole at right front edge: Rib 3, make buttonhole, rib to end of row.

Complete as for left front, reversing all shapings and working buttonholes to correspond with the button placement on the left band.

Adjust length of the buttonhole band and stitch in place.

At center back neck weave the sts of the two bands together, or BO the sts and seam neatly.

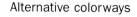

Alternative colorways

Vest Variation

This vest is a simple variation of the cardigan pattern and is amazingly quick to knit. I designed it with my sister-in-law in mind: She's a school teacher with a great sense of fun, hence the choice of buttons for the closures as well as the embellishments for this vest. Watch out though—your friends may suddenly start bringing you "gifts" of buttons that just happen to reflect their hobbies and interests!

MATERIALS

10 (11, 12, 13, 14) balls Plymouth Yarn Company's Dakota (50 g = 80 m)

Knitting needles in size 8 and 10 (5 and 6 mm) or size needed to give correct gauge

24- or 29-inch (61 or 74 cm) circular knitting needle in size 8 (5 mm)

5 buttons

FRONT AND BACK

Knit the back and the fronts exactly the same as for the cardigan.

Join shoulder seams.

Work button and buttonhole bands as for the cardigan.

Add pockets if desired as directed in the cardigan instructions.

SLEEVE BANDS

With right sides facing and using the circular needle, pick up and knit sts between the markers for sleeve bands. Working 1 st in from the edge, pick up 2 sts for every 3 rows. Check that you have an equal number of sts on both sides of the shoulder seam. (Hint: To get a rough idea of the number of sts to pick up, hold the armhole edge against the ribbed band of the back and count the number of sts.)

Work 1 to 1½ inches (2.5 to 4 cm) in K1P1 rib.

BO all sts.

Join sleeve band and side seams.

Cardigan with Knit-In Front Bands

This quick-knit cardigan features front bands that are simply knit in (as opposed to forming the band by picking up stitches) as you go along.

STITCH PATTERNS

Garter stitch = every row knit

Reverse stocking stitch = the wrong side of stockinette st

BACK

Using smaller needles, cast on 58 (64, 70, 74) sts.

Work 8 rows in garter st (this will give you 4 ridges).

Change to larger needles and work in rev St st until back measures 22 (23, 24, 25) inches (56, 58.5, 61, 63.5 cm).

Begin shoulder shaping: BO 6 (7, 8, 8) at beg of next 2 rows, then 6 (7, 8, 9) at beg of following 2 rows and 7 (8, 8, 9) at beg of last 2 rows.

BO remaining 20 (20, 22, 22) back neck sts.

Place markers 9 (9½, 10½, 11) inches (23, 24, 27, 28 cm) down from beginning of shoulder shaping to indicate armhole.

SIZES

Small (medium, large, extra large)

FINISHED MEASUREMENTS

Chest: 39 (43, 47, 49) inches (99, 109, 119.5, 124.5 cm)

MATERIALS

16 (16, 17, 17) balls of Berroco's Déjà Vu (50 g = approximately 48 m)

Knitting needles in size 7 and 9 (4.5 and 5.5 mm) or size needed to obtain correct gauge

5 buttons

GAUGE

12 sts and 18 rows = 4 inches (10 cm) in reverse stockinette stitch (rev St st)

LEFT FRONT

Using smaller needles, cast on 35 (38, 41, 43) sts, noting that 6 sts will form the border.

Work 8 rows garter st.

Change to larger needles.

Next row: Right side facing, purl to last 6 sts, knit 6.

Next row: Knit.

Continue working in rev St st, remembering to work 6 sts in garter st at front edge on every row. (Place a marker to remind you if necessary.)

Knit until the work measures 12 (12, 12, 12) inches (31 cm)

BEGIN NECK SHAPING:

With right sides of work facing, work to last 8 sts. K2tog, knit 6.

Repeat every 4 rows until 25 (28, 30, 32) sts remain and at the same time, when the piece measures same as back to start of shoulder shaping, work shoulder as you did for the back.

Continue knitting on 6 remaining front band sts for about 3½ inches (9 cm). Place sts on safety pin.

Mark position of buttons on the left front band, placing the first half an inch (12 mm) from the bottom, and last just below the start of neck shaping. Space the rest of the markers evenly in between—this is easy to do, just count the number of garter st ridges.

RIGHT FRONT

Knit as for the left, reversing all shaping, remembering to work the button holes to correspond with the markers.

SLEEVES

Using smaller needles, cast on 26 (28, 28, 30) sts and work 8 rows garter st.

Change to larger needles and rev St st.

Work increases as follows: Inc 1 st on each side of the knitting every 4 rows until there are 54 (58, 64, 66) sts on the needle.

Work straight until the sleeve measures 17 (17½, 18, 18½) inches (43, 44.5, 46, 47 cm).

Adjust sleeve length if necessary here.

BO sts loosely.

FINISHING
Using a smooth yarn in a matching color, sew shoulder seams together.

Adjust length of garter st borders to meet in center back neck.

Bind off sts and seam together neatly.

St border neatly to back neck.

Pin sleeve in position between the markers and stitch to armhole.

Complete side and sleeve seams.

Sew on the buttons to correspond with the buttonholes.

Go dazzle the world!

Close-up view of knit-in front bands

Schematics for Cardigan

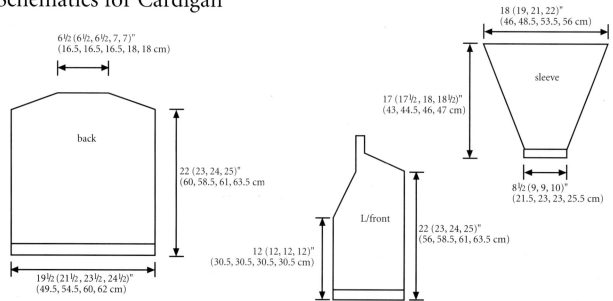

6½ (6½, 6½, 7, 7)"
(16.5, 16.5, 16.5, 18, 18 cm)

back

22 (23, 24, 25)"
(60, 58.5, 61, 63.5 cm

19½ (21½, 23½, 24½)"
(49.5, 54.5, 60, 62 cm)

L/front

12 (12, 12, 12)"
(30.5, 30.5, 30.5, 30.5 cm)

22 (23, 24, 25)"
(56, 58.5, 61, 63.5 cm)

18 (19, 21, 22)"
(46, 48.5, 53.5, 56 cm)

sleeve

17 (17½, 18, 18½)"
(43, 44.5, 46, 47 cm)

8½ (9, 9, 10)"
(21.5, 23, 23, 25.5 cm)

Loose Line Garter Stitch Jacket

This colorful, lightweight jacket was inspired by the spectacular beauty of the spring wildflowers in Texas. The knitting is all garter stitch so it goes quickly and easily. You can leave your jacket without an edge finish as the beauty of garter stitch is that it lies flat and does not need any other finish, but the contrasting bands give the cardigan an elegant, tailored look.

Photo: Texas Parks & Wildlife

SIZES
Petite (small, medium, large, extra large)

FINISHED MEASUREMENTS
Bust: 37 (41, 43, 47, 51) inches (94, 104, 109, 119.5, 129.5 cm)

Length: 24 (25, 26, 27, 28) inches (61, 63.5, 66, 68.5, 71 cm)

MATERIALS
15 (15, 16, 16, 17) balls in #525 (A) of Plymouth Yarn Company's Filati Bertagna Ciao (50 g = approximately 100 m)

1 ball for all sizes in #56 (B) Galway 100% virgin wool (100 g = 230 yds) worsted weight

Knitting needles in size 9 and 8 (5.5 and 5.0 mm) or size needed to give correct gauge

Circular knitting needle in size 8 (5.0 mm)

GAUGE
16 sts and 32 rows = 4 inches (10 cm)

This gauge means that there are 4 sts and 8 rows to the inch. Remember that every 2 rows knitted gives one ridge of garter stitch. In other words, your gauge is 4 sts and 4 ridges to the inch, using size 9 (5.5 mm) needles.

STITCH PATTERN
Garter stitch = every row knit

A NOTE ON YARN SUBSTITUTION:
The yarn used for this jacket knits up into a very striking fabric. For best results when substituting yarn, choose a textured yarn with variegated colors.

BACK

Using larger needles and A, cast on 74 (82, 86, 94,102) sts.

Work in garter stitch until piece measures 15 (15½, 16, 16, 16½) inches (38, 39.5, 40.5, 40.5, 42 cm).

Shape armhole: BO 4 (4, 4, 6, 6) at beginning of next 2 rows so that 66 (74, 78, 82, 90) sts remain.

Continue knitting until piece measures 24 (25, 26, 27, 28) inches (61, 63.5, 66, 68.5, 71 cm).

BO all sts.

LEFT FRONT

Using larger needles and A, cast on 39 (43, 45, 49, 53) sts and knit as for back to armhole shaping.

With right side facing BO 4 (4, 4, 6, 6) sts to leave 35 (39, 41, 43, 47) sts.

Knit to last 3 sts, k2tog, k1.

Continue decreasing 1 st at neck edge every 6 rows until 24 (28, 29, 32, 35) sts remain.

Work straight until front measures the same as back in length.

BO all sts.

RIGHT FRONT

As left, reversing all shapings.

SLEEVES

Using larger needles and A, cast on 34 (36, 38, 40, 44) sts.

Work in garter stitch, increasing 1 st at each end of sleeve every 6 rows until there are 72 (76, 80, 88, 92) sts on the needle.

Work straight until sleeve measures 17½ (18, 18½, 19, 19½) inches (44.5, 46, 47, 48.5, 49.5 cm).

BO sts.

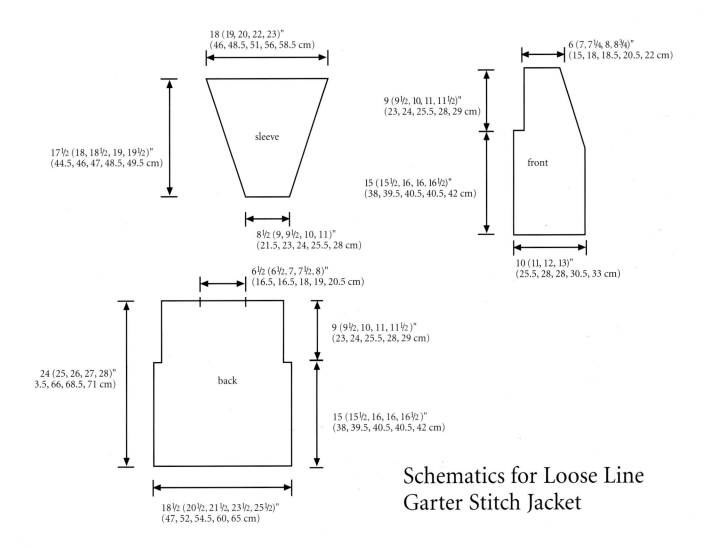

Schematics for Loose Line Garter Stitch Jacket

FINISHING

Stitch back and fronts together at shoulders.

Take a look at the photos and decide which edging you would like to use for your jacket. The jacket shown here has a rolled edge. After you have finished your edging, sew the sleeve and side seams together carefully.

EDGE FINISHES

For all the edge finishes, use B and circular needles. With right side facing start at lower edge of the right front and pick up one stitch for each ridge up to the shoulder seam.

Pick up 26 (26, 28, 30, 32) sts across the back neck and continue picking up 1 st for every ridge down to the left lower edge. Check that you have an equal number of sts on each front edge.

EDGE #1: REVERSE STOCKINETTE STITCH ROLL Work in St st for about an inch (2.5 cm). Cast off loosely. The purl side of the band will roll beautifully to the front edge of the jacket.

EDGE #3: K2P2 RIB
Work for about 1 inch (2.5 cm) and cast off in the rib stitch.

EDGE #2: HEMMED BORDER
Knit about an inch (2.5 cm) in stocking stitch. With purl side facing, knit one row. This makes a turning ridge. Continue knitting in St st for the same number of rows. Cast off loosely. Fold and hem band into place. The band will lie very neatly because of the difference in weight and texture of the two knitted fabrics.

EDGE #4: PIPED EDGE
This is a firm edge which resembles crochet and is very easy to do. Simply pick up the stitches, knit 1 row, and BO again in the next row.

Patchwork Jacket

Patchwork knitting has solved many of my "what-shall-I-take-along-to-knit?" dilemmas and led to some striking garments. The rectangles are quick to knit and look so tempting when they are stacked up in little heaps; they practically beg you to turn them into something! Don't limit yourself to making a jacket from them—vests, pockets, cuffs, hats, and scarves are other great choices.

MATERIALS

Approximately 4 skeins of Mountain Colors ⁴⁄₈s wool (4 oz =112 g)

Needles in your choice of size

Gridded dressmaker's pattern paper (available at fabric and quilting stores)

Safety pins

Tapestry needle

☞ **TIP:** Buy each skein a different color, as the variegation within each will give you a far greater color range.

GAUGE

Gauge is not important here. It's only your gauge that matters and this can vary considerably if you are using a variety of weights and textures. Even if you make all your patchwork pieces 20 stitches, the variety of sizes will be that much more interesting.

MAKING THE RECTANGLES

Cast on 20 stitches and work in box stitch. Rows 1 and 2: K2P2 to end. Rows 3 and 4: P2K2 to end. (My rectangles measure 4 x 3 inches [10 x 7.5 cm], but they can be any size.) I don't add seam stitches as these will be pieced together both vertically and horizontally, but be sure to leave yourself a few inches (5 to 7.5 cm) of your cast on/bind off threads to use in sewing up.

ASSEMBLING THE GARMENT

So how will you put a garment together from these lovely rectangles? First, you will need a pattern piece to put your modules on. Cut a template from freezer paper, craft paper or from gridded dressmaker's pattern paper. This is my paper of choice, available at fabric stores and quilting stores. You can pin the pieces easily onto it and then drape the work-in-progress on yourself.

Look at the schematic on page 49 to give you an idea of how to proceed. Using your gridded paper, mark off the appropriate number of inches or centimeters. Cut a piece for the back, for the fronts, and for the sleeves. Use an existing sweater that fits you well, and draw the shape of its pieces or choose a schematic from a knitting pattern you like and proceed from there. If you are unsure, make a simple vest shape.

Use safety pins to fasten your rectangles onto the pattern pieces. You can pin rectangles all around the outer edges and work inward, or work from the center out, arranging the pieces like a jigsaw puzzle. Gaps can be filled in by knitting the missing piece, or pick up stitches and knit on to an existing rectangle. You may need to shape an area by increasing or decreasing, but this is very easily done, particularly as knitting is such a flexible fabric. By the way, no law says the edges of the garment must be straight—look at

the sketches and see how interesting a jacket can look when the edges are uneven.

When each of your garment pieces is about filled up, safety pin them together to get a rough idea of how it will look. Take care not to stretch your rectangles. Start sewing them together, working with the right side facing to avoid bulky seams. Don't be afraid. Nothing can go wrong. At the worst, you'll have to unpick a rectangle or two.

Edge finishes may be left as they are because the modules lie flat and the edges are neat. This makes it easy to pick up stitches where desired, to knit on ribbing for cuffs and welts, or to add other areas of knitting. Use a suitable yarn and needles and see where this leads you. The illustrations provided may give you some ideas, but experiment—nothing is carved in stone. This is your project; you have full control of it. So

what if the piece you added on doesn't look right? Pull the knitting out gently and try again.

Consider how the finished garment might look. Do you want a solid contrast color? Sometimes this can rcally sct off a piece but it can also be too sharp a contrast. I have found that narrow bands of solid color work best. (The jacket shown here has not had any bands or edgings added.)

Patchwork Jacket Schematics

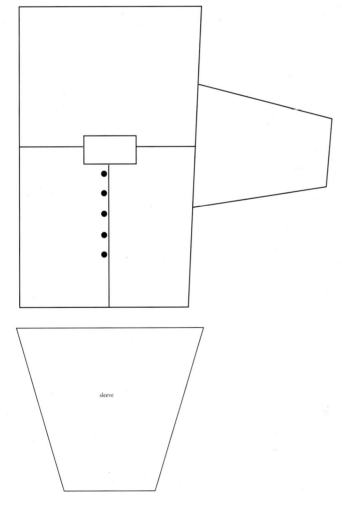

Arranging the rectangles

Design Variations

Patchwork areas can be incorporated in the design of just about any type of knitwear. Here are a few ideas—let your imagination go and design your own variations.

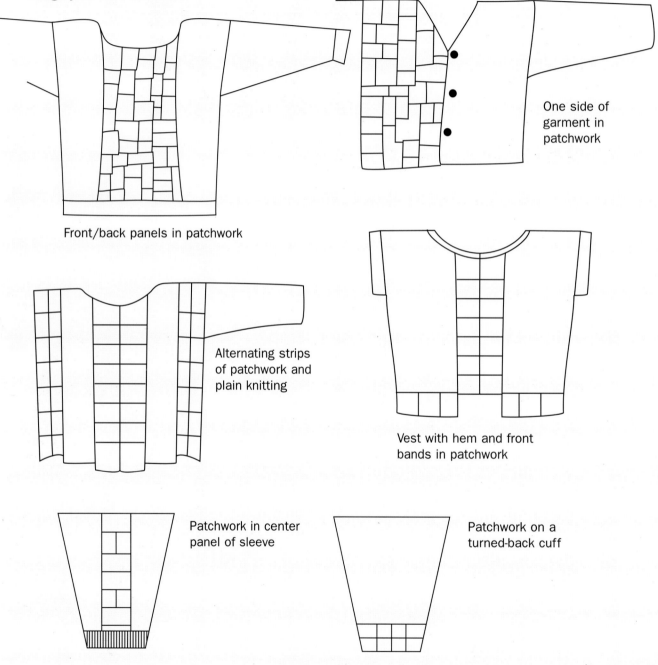

Front/back panels in patchwork

One side of garment in patchwork

Alternating strips of patchwork and plain knitting

Vest with hem and front bands in patchwork

Patchwork in center panel of sleeve

Patchwork on a turned-back cuff

Work in progress using different weights and textures of yarn

Knitting on the Go

Having just the right project to knit while traveling or waiting was often a problem, as I always seemed to be at some crucial stage in a project where I had to concentrate or hadn't packed the right needles.

I grew tired of knitting hats, and much as I love to knit socks, the knitting often got fiddly. Then came the time I dropped a sock needle on a plane! (Never did find it and it has no doubt earned itself millions of award miles by now, wedged in some crevice.) One day,

while rushing to pack something to knit on a cross-country flight, I grabbed a gorgeous skein of Mountain Colors yarn, tossed in needles of appropriate size, along with my knitting essentials bag and roared off. I always make swatches on sock needles as I find them easier to handle. I soon found myself knitting a 20-stitch swatch. The yarn was so seductive that soon there were several little rectangles in various stitch patterns. The variegated yarn made each rectangle look a little different. When I returned home I selected more skeins, kept on knitting rectangles at odd moments, and the jacket on page 48 was the result.

This type of knitting led to the creation of what I call my diplo-

matic pouches. If you prepare a few of these pouches you will always have a tiny project ready for those odd moments, and the pieces soon add up. To make a diplomatic pouch, place a pair of sock needles in a zippered pouch or small cosmetic bag. (Sock needles come in sets of 4 or 5, so one set will allow you to prepare two bags.) Add a small pair of scissors or snips and a few small balls of yarn wound off from skeins. Needle size is not really too big of a deal—just put in something appropriate for the yarn. Pop these into your purse or tote and keep one in a travel bag. These rectangles are so portable, so unobtrusive, and easily done where you might not want to be seen knitting.

VESTS

Vests may well be the most versatile item in a wardrobe. They can pull an outfit together, keep you warm, or function purely as adornment. They layer so beautifully and can be worn by any figure type. One can simply never have enough of them!

Basic Vest

This is a really basic, bread-and-butter vest pattern and it comes to you in seven sizes. You may make the vest longer or shorter if you prefer. Try a touch of embroidery or change button placings. Something as simple as color and button choices will take this pattern from the chic and sophisticated through the casual to the truly wild. (Refer to the chapter on embellishment.) The wool bouclé yarn chosen for the vest shown here features a light, fluffy texture which gives the fabric some surface interest. It's also a good choice of yarn if you are a little uncertain about achieving an even gauge. Either side of the knitting can be used as the right side. Ideas for changing the look of the vest are given at the end of the instructions.

SIZES

To fit bust 32 (34, 36, 38, 40, 42, 44) inches (81, 86.5, 91.5, 96.5, 101.5, 107, 112 cm)

FINISHED MEASUREMENTS

Bust: 37 (39, 41, 43, 45, 47, 49) inches (94, 99, 104, 109, 114.5, 119.5, 124.5 cm)

Length: 21 (21, 21, 22½, 22½, 24, 24) inches (53.5, 53.5, 53.5, 57, 57, 61, 61 cm)

MATERIALS

6 (6, 7, 7, 8, 8, 8) skeins of Brown Sheep Company's Fantasy Lace 100% Wool Bouclé (50 g = 1.75 oz; approximately 96 yds = 86.5 m)

Knitting needles in size 6 and 8 (4 mm and 5 mm) or size to obtain gauge

Circular needle in size 6 (4 mm)

Buttons

GAUGE

14 sts = 4 inches (10 cm) measured over St st with larger needles

BACK

Using smaller needles, cast on 60 (62, 66, 68, 72, 74, 78) sts and work in K1P1 rib for 2 inches (5 cm). On the last row, increase 6 (6, 6, 8, 8, 8, 8) sts, evenly spaced, across the row. You will have 66 (68, 72, 76, 80, 82, 86) sts.

Change to larger needles and work in St st until piece measures 12 (12, 12, 13, 13, 14, 14) inches (30.5, 30.5, 30.5, 33, 33, 35.5, 35.5 cm).

Armhole shaping: BO 5 (5, 6, 6, 7, 7, 8) sts at beginning of next two rows. Decrease 1 st at each side every alternate row 4 (5, 5, 6, 7, 7, 7) times until 48 (48, 50, 52, 52, 54, 56) sts remain. Continue knitting until the back measures 21 (21, 21, 22½, 22½, 24, 24) inches (53.5, 53.5, 53.5, 57, 57, 61, 61 cm).

Reverse side of knitting

Shoulder shaping: BO 6 (6, 6, 7, 7, 7, 7) sts at the beg of the next 2 rows, then BO 6 (6, 7, 7, 7, 7, 8) sts at beg of following 2 rows. Place the remaining 24 (24, 24, 24, 24, 26, 26) back neck sts on a holder.

LEFT FRONT

With smaller needles, cast on 30 (31, 33, 34, 36, 37, 39) sts and work in rib as for back, increasing 3 (3, 3, 4, 4, 4, 4) sts evenly across the row which will give you a total of 33 (34, 36, 38, 40, 41, 43) sts.

Change to larger needles and work as for back to start of armhole shaping, ending with right side facing.

Shape neck and armhole: Shape armhole as for back, and at the same time decrease 1 st at neck edge on the next and every following 3rd row until 12 (12, 13, 14, 14, 14, 15) sts remain.

Continue knitting until the piece measures the same as the back to start of shoulder shaping, ending with the right side facing. BO 6, (6, 6, 7, 7, 7, 7) sts at beg of next row. Purl 1 rowl BO 6 (6, 7, 7, 7, 7, 8) sts.

RIGHT FRONT

Work to match left front, reversing all shapings.

FINISHING

Block pieces carefully.

Join shoulder seams.

Arm bands: Using smaller needles, pick up and knit approximately 84 (84, 84, 88, 88, 94, 94) sts evenly around the armhole edge.

Work in K1P1 rib for 1 inch (2.5 cm).

BO loosely in rib.

Mark position for buttons on the left front, placing the first marker

½ inch (1.5 cm) below the start of the front neck shaping and the last ½ inch (1.5 cm) above the cast-on edge.

Space the other buttons evenly in between.

Front bands: Using circular needle and with right side facing, start at lower right front edge, pick up and knit approximately 200 (200, 200, 212, 212, 226, 226) sts all around the edges and down to the lower left front edge. (Refer to pages 19 and for a review of picking up sts.)

Work 3 rows in K1P1 rib.

Next row (buttonhole row) work button holes to correspond with the marked positions of the buttons.

Work 3 more rows.

BO in rib.

Sew the side seams.

Sew on buttons.

Schematics for Basic Vest

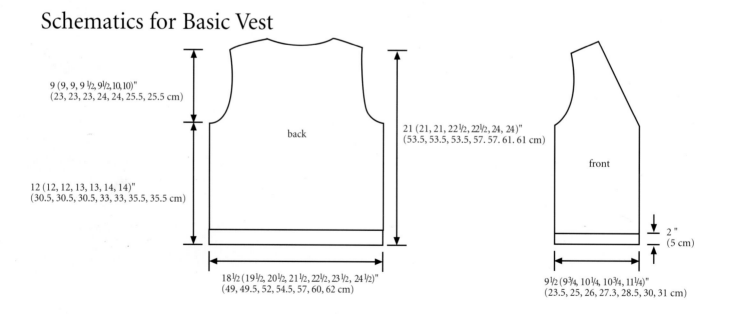

9 (9, 9, 9 ½, 9½, 10, 10)"
(23, 23, 23, 24, 24, 25.5, 25.5 cm)

back

21 (21, 21, 22½, 22½, 24, 24)"
(53.5, 53.5, 53.5, 57. 57. 61. 61 cm)

front

12 (12, 12, 13, 13, 14, 14)"
(30.5, 30.5, 30.5, 33, 33, 35.5, 35.5 cm)

2 "
(5 cm)

18½ (19½, 20½, 21½, 22½, 23½, 24½)"
(49, 49.5, 52, 54.5, 57, 60, 62 cm)

9½ (9¾, 10¼, 10¾, 11¼)"
(23.5, 25, 26, 27.3, 28.5, 30, 31 cm)

Variations

You can easily change the look of this vest using the same basic pattern. Some suggestions:

- Change the basic K1P1 rib. For example, try moss stitch for the bands.
- Knit the body in stripes; knit the bands in stripes.
- Do a little color blocking.
- For a more casual look, omit the lower rib bands, cast on with smaller needles, work a few rows in St st, change to larger needles, and continue.

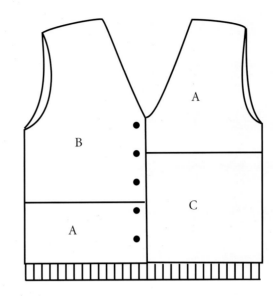

Color blocked

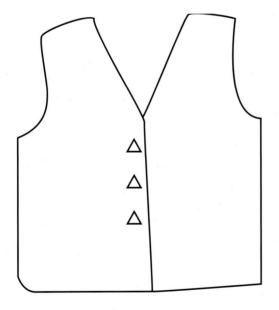

Rolled stockinette edge

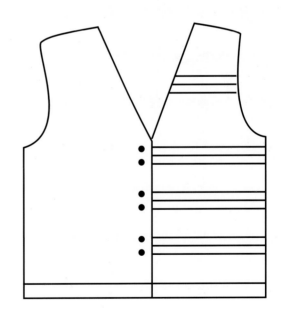

Stripe variations

Indian Vest

The design for this simple, understated vest was loosely based on garments worn in Indian sub-continent cultures. The distinctive arm bands are knit in as you work in garter stitch.

SIZES
Small (medium, large)

FINISHED MEASUREMENTS
Bust: 36 (40, 44)

MATERIALS
6 (7, 7) skeins Classic Elite's 25% mohair 75% wool Tapestry (1 skein = 50 g [1.75 oz], approximately 95 yds [85.5 m])

Needles in size 6 and 8 (4 and 5 mm) or size to obtain gauge

Embellishments of choice

GAUGE
18 sts = 4 inches (10 cm) measured over St st on larger needles

BACK
Using smaller needles, cast on 80 (88, 98) sts and knit 12 rows (6 garter st ridges).

Change to larger needles and work in St st for 10 (10½, 11) inches (25.5, 27, 28 cm) ending with wrong side facing.

*Knit 8 (9, 11) sts, purl to the last 8 (9, 11) sts, knit. *

Knit the next row.

Repeat from * to *.

Shape armholes (right side facing): BO 5 (6, 8) sts, knit to the end of the row. BO 5 (6, 8) sts, knit 3, purl to last 3 sts, knit 3. Next row, knit 3, ssk, knit to last 5 sts, k2tog, knit 3. Next row knit 3, purl to last 3 sts, knit 3. Continue decreasing at armhole for a total of 5 (6, 7) decreases maintaining 3 sts in garter st until 60 (64, 68) sts remain.

Continue knitting, remembering to keep 3 sts in garter st on each armhole edge until the back measures 18½ (19½, 20½) inches (47, 49.5, 52 cm).

Shape shoulders: BO 5 (5, 6) sts at beg of next two rows. BO 5 (6, 6) sts at beg of next two rows. BO 6 (6, 6) sts at beg of next two rows. Leave remaining 28 (30, 32) sts on a holder.

LEFT FRONT
Using smaller needles, cast on 40 (44, 49) sts.

Work as given for the back, including the armhole shaping (when armhole shaping is complete you will have 30 [32, 34] sts).

When the work measures 14 (15, 16) inches from the beg, start neck shaping.

Shape neck: With the wrong side facing purl 12 (13, 14) sts. Leave these sts on a holder and purl to the last 3 sts, k3. Maintaining the garter st border at the armhole edge, decrease 1 st at the neck edge every alternate row twice. Continue working on these remaining 16 (17, 18) sts until the front measures the same as the back to the start of the shoulder shaping. Work shoulder shaping as for back.

RIGHT FRONT
Work as given for the Left Front, reversing all shapings.

FINISHING
Block pieces carefully. (See page OO for a review of blocking techniques.) Join shoulder seams.

With right side facing and smaller needles, pick up and knit approximately 74 (78, 82) sts around the neck, including the sts left on holders.

Work in garter st for ½ inch (1.5 cm).

BO sts.

BUTTON BAND
With smaller needles and right side facing, begin at top of neckband and pick up 2 sts for every 3 rows along the left front edge, end-

ing immediately above the garter st bottom band.

Working in garter st knit 10 more rows.

BO the sts.

Mark the position of the buttons as desired.

BUTTONHOLE BAND
With right side facing and smaller needles, pick up sts as for button band.

Work button holes to correspond with your markers on the 5th row as follows: knit to position of the buttonhole, yfw, k2tog.

Knit 5 more rows.

BO.

Join side seams.

Sew on buttons.

Embellish as desired.

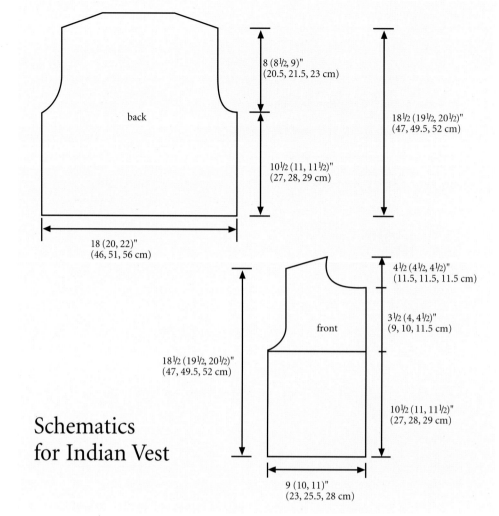

8 (8½, 9)"
(20.5, 21.5, 23 cm)

10½ (11, 11½)"
(27, 28, 29 cm)

18 (20, 22)"
(46, 51, 56 cm)

back

18½ (19½, 20½)"
(47, 49.5, 52 cm)

4½ (4½, 4½)"
(11.5, 11.5, 11.5 cm)

3½ (4, 4½)"
(9, 10, 11.5 cm)

front

18½ (19½, 20½)"
(47, 49.5, 52 cm)

10½ (11, 11½)"
(27, 28, 29 cm)

9 (10, 11)"
(23, 25.5, 28 cm)

Schematics
for Indian Vest

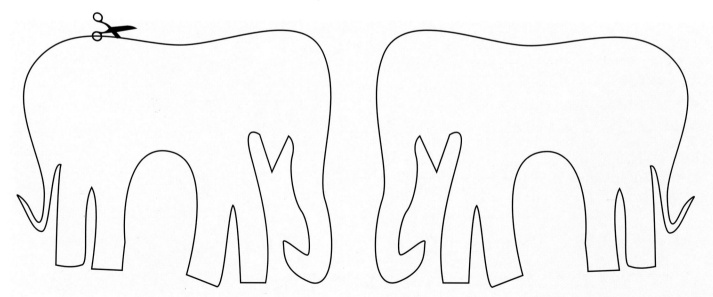

Appliqué pattern

Variation

This vest was inspired from the centuries-old traditions of embroidery and embellishment in India. Very simple embroidery techniques—chain stitch, stem stitch, running stitch, and others—are used to beautiful advantage in Indian embroidery, especially if you choose stranded floss, metallic threads, or decorative novelty yarns. For embellishment, use beads, tiny buttons (particularly mother-of-pearl), and pieces from dismantled jewelry.

MATERIALS
Red and black felt scraps
Embroidery floss and needle
Buttons

Cut 10 1½-inch (4 cm) squares from the red felt and pin them around the bottom edge of the vest. Secure in place with a buttonhole stitch, then sew a button in the center of the square.

Cut two elephants from the black felt using the pattern on page 60. Pin in position and secure with buttonhole stitch.

Textured Vest

This vest style features a dropped shoulder and is knit sideways to create flattering vertical lines. The beautiful color and texture changes are created by working with a variety of yarns. If you don't already have a stash of novelty yarns, look for gorgeous balls in sale bins or sweet-talk your knitting friends into sharing their leftovers. Also, don't overlook the very fine yarns or the glitzy embroidery threads—they look wonderful when two strands are held together as one.

SIZES AND FINISHED MEASUREMENTS
There is no set pattern for this vest. The size and finished measurements of the vest will be determined by taking a few simple measurements from a favorite, well-fitting sweater.

MATERIALS
Approximately 1 pound total of an interesting assortment of background and novelty yarns. This vest uses worsted-weight mohair/wool blend yarn as the main yarn and novelty metallic, glitter, and eyelash yarns for accents.

Needle size suited to your test gauge.

GAUGE
Determine the gauge by knitting a 6-inch-square (15 cm) swatch from the yarn you have the most of. Measure the swatch carefully to establish the number of stitches per inch.

PATTERN STITCH
Garter stitch rows of novelty yarns are broken up with several rows of stockinette in background yarn.

Note: It is especially important in this project to cast on and off loosely.

BACK
Measure the back of a favorite sweater across the shoulders and then measure for length. Multiply your length measurement by your gauge and you have the number of sts to cast on.

Cast on and start knitting the back. For this vest, rows of garter stitch in novelty yarns were broken up with several rows of stockinette in the background yarn. Continue knitting until the seam measures your desired back width, without stretching.

Decide on the back neck width by measuring that favorite sweater. It will probably be somewhere around 7 inches (18 cm). Subtract this measurement from the total back width, divide the result by two, and you have the width of each shoulder piece. This measurement will also be the width for each front piece.

FRONT
Cast on the same number of sts as for the back and knit two front pieces to the required width, working again from side to side. Note: I do not make these front pieces identical, though you may of course, as I really enjoy the more spontaneous look of the fabric.

FINISHING

Sew the shoulder seams together. You are now at the point of deciding about bands.

Place markers on the front and back pieces at the point where you want the underarm seam to begin. As this is a drop-shoulder style, you probably don't want your armhole opening to be less than 8 inches (20 cm).

Decide on the yarn and needle size to use, then pick up an even number of sts on front and back for the arm bands. Work about 1 inch (2.5 cm) in K1P1 rib. Cast off.

Complete the underarm seam.

☛ **TIP:** Sew from the underarm to the bottom of the garment as this prevents the seam from being pulled up.

Try your vest on and consider how you might do the rest of the finishing. Does it need a bottom band? If so, place safety pins as markers at the side seams, at center back, and space a few others evenly in between. Using a circular needle, pick up and knit sts around the hem, using the pins as guides so that you obtain a more or less equal no of sts between markers. Work the band in rib as you did the sleeves. Or try this:

Knit one row after the picking up row, and then cast off.

This brings you to the front bands. With a circular needle and right side facing, pick up sts from the bottom edge, along the right front, across the back neck, and down the left front, then proceed as for the other bands.

If you prefer to knit the band separately, cast on a few sts for a band about 1½ inches (4 cm) wide and knit until it is long enough to go all the way around the front edges. Sew neatly into place.

Schematics for Textured Vest

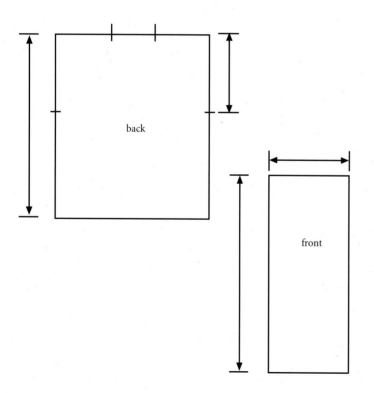

back

front

Shawl

A shawl is a great way to become comfortable with free-style knitting. Start with a selection of yarns in luscious colors and fabulous textures.

MATERIALS

Approximately 1 pound total of an interesting assortment of yarns. Be sure to include several balls of novelty yarns.

A circular needle in a size appropriate for your yarns (Note: Since you will be mixing yarns of different weights and textures, choose a needle size quite a lot bigger than you might ordinarily use; I tend to use a 10 or 10 ½ [6·or 6½ mm].)

GAUGE

Gauge is not crucial here, but you do want your shawl to have a nice drape.

TO BEGIN

Cast on 3 sts

Row 1: K3

Row 2: KI, inc 1 st, K1, inc 1 st, K1. You now have 5 sts.

Mark the center st.

Row 3: K5

Row 4: Inc 1 st, knit to marked st, inc 1 st, knit the marked st, make next inc, knit to last st, inc 1 = 9 sts.

Row 5: Knit

Repeat rows 4 and 5 throughout.

You will soon see how the shaping progresses and that you are increasing a total of 4 sts, every alternate row. Now the fun part begins!

You can join in the new yarns at either end of a row or in the middle. Work several rows of stockinette here and there, then alternate a few purl sts with knit sts. This is your fabric, in your colors and in your size. Not much can go wrong. So knit away, joining in new yarns as the fancy takes you. You can either darn in the loose ends when you are finished knitting (something which I find relaxing to do) or work the ends in as you go along.

You should always have an odd number of sts, or looked at another way, an equal no of sts either side of the marked st. But what if you suddenly find you forgot one of the side increases somewhere? This is no biggie—the colors and textures are so varied it can never be noticed. Just balance it out in the next row so you will have an even number of sts either side of the marked st.

A NOTE ON INCREASES

You can make your increases in the first and last sts at the side edges if you like, but I prefer to do mine one st in from the edge—it makes for a neater edge. There are many ways to do the increases on either side of the marked center st. If you want a decorative row of holes in the center of your shawl, knit to the marked st, lift up the thread lying between this last knitted st and the marked st, and knit it. Then knit the marked st and make the second increase between it and the next st in the same way. If you would rather not have this decorative increase, place the lifted thread onto the left needle and knit into the back of it.

At some point you will need to decide how big you are going to make the shawl. My advice is not to skimp on it. You want your shawl to make a statement, so knit until you are satisfied. If you are unsure about the length of your shawl, thread a large tapestry needle with a smooth yarn in a contrasting color and take all the sts off your knitting needle. Spread it out to its full size and delight in your work. Is it long enough? Will a fringe bring it up to the right length? Replace the stitches and continue knitting or cast off loosely.

If you choose to add a fringe, make it a generous one. Cut yarns twice the length of the finished fringe, fold in half, and use a crochet hook to draw them though the edges of the shawl. Start by placing a fringe on each corner, and then space the rest evenly along the two sides.

What if you notice a row of color that doesn't seem to work? Just embellish it by making a few bobbles, adding tiny buttons, tying in little bits of other yarn, or by threading a needle with a contrasting color of yarn and working some running stitches.

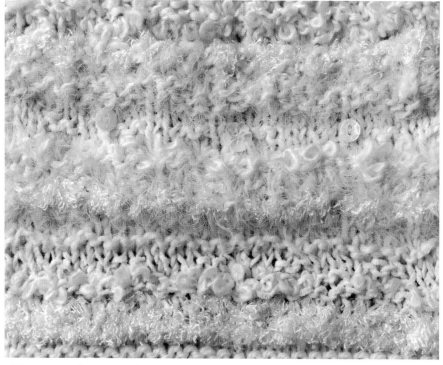

Alternate colorway embellished with rows of small buttons

Shawl Collar Vest

The pattern stitch for this vest is very easy to knit and results in a reversible fabric which lies flat, needing no other edge finishing. What could be simpler? You can wear it open or fastened edge-to-edge.

SIZES
Small (medium, large)

FINISHED MEASUREMENTS
Bust: 38 (42, 46) inches (96.5, 107, 117 cm)

Length: 19 (19½, 20) inches (48.5, 50, 51 cm)

MATERIALS
3 (3, 4) skeins (1 skein = 4 oz, 112 g) Mountain Colors hand-painted merino ribbon yarn (80% super fine merino wool, 20% nylon)

Knitting needles in size 9 (5.5 mm) or size needed to obtain gauge

GAUGE
16 sts = 4 inches (10 cm) over pattern stitch

Pattern Stitch (this is called Box Stitch)

1st row: K2 *P2K2. Repeat from * to end of row.

2nd row: P2 *K2P2. Repeat from * to end of row.

3rd row: P2 *K2P2. Repeat from * to end of row.

4th row: K2 *P2K2. Repeat from * to end of row.

Repeat these four rows.

BACK
Cast on 78 (86, 94) sts and work in pattern st until the piece measures 18 (18½, 19) inches (46, 47, 48.5 cm).

SHOULDER SHAPING
BO 6 (7, 8) sts at beg of next 8 rows.

BO the remaining 30 sts.

FRONTS
(NOTE: You may reverse shapings, or simply work both pieces alike since the fabric is reversible.)

Cast on 42 (46, 50) sts and work in pattern st until the piece meas-

ures the same as the back to start of shoulder shaping.

With right side facing, shape shoulder as for back.

There will be 18 (18, 18) sts remaining.

For all sizes, continue working in pattern on these sts for a further 4½ (4½, 4½) inches (11.5, 11.5, 11.5 cm).

BO loosely.

FINISHING
Place markers on fronts and back 8 (8½, 9) inches (20.5, 21.5, 23 cm) from start of shoulder shaping.

Join shoulder seams.

Join ends of collar, remembering that wrong side of collar will be on the right side of garment.

Stitch collar to the back neck edge.

Join side seams below the markers.

Apply closure/buttons if desired. Note: The clasp for this vest was designed by bead artist Geri Omohundro.

Schematics for Shawl Collar Vest

The brilliant hues in this velvety yarn reflect memories of the Aegean Sea along the Pelion Peninsula in Greece.

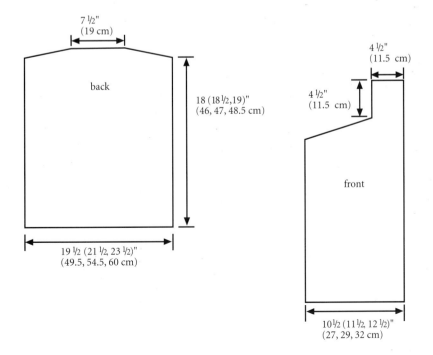

7 ½"
(19 cm)

back

18 (18 ½, 19)"
(46, 47, 48.5 cm)

19 ½ (21 ½, 23 ½)"
(49.5, 54.5, 60 cm)

4 ½"
(11.5 cm)

4 ½"
(11.5 cm)

front

10 ½ (11 ½, 12 ½)"
(27, 29, 32 cm)

TOPS

All of the top designs in this chapter are very simple to make. Tops like these use only a few balls of yarn, so you can splurge on really fabulous yarns without great expense to produce an array of garments for your wardrobe.

Extra Quick Rolled-Hem Top

The simple design of this cropped top can see you through a number of occasions: wear it to the office by day, then reach into your tote for that stunning pin or the ethnic necklace which is one of your signature pieces. Just change your shoes and the evening is yours. The front and back pieces are alike and the yarn is bulky so the knitting really goes quickly.

SIZES

Petite (small, medium, large)

Finished Measurements

Bust: 39 (41, 43, 45) inches (99, 104, 109, 114.5 cm)

Body length: 19 (20, 20, 21) inches (48.5, 51, 51, 53.5 cm)

Sleeve length: 14 (14, 15, 15) inches (35.5, 35.5, 38, 38 cm)

MATERIALS

11 (12, 12, 14) balls (1 ball = 55 yds, 50 g) in main color and 1 (1, 2, 2) balls in contrast color in Berroco's Pronto (50% cotton, 50% acrylic)

Knitting needles in sizes 10 and 10½ (6 mm and 6.5 mm) or size to obtain gauge

Circular needle in size 10 (6 mm)

GAUGE

13 sts and 19 rows = 4 inches (10 cm) measured over St st with larger needles

BACK AND FRONT
(they are identical)

Using smaller needles and contrast color, cast on 64 (68, 70, 74) sts and work 6 rows in St st.

Change to larger needles and main color and continue until the work measures 10 (10½, 10½, 11) inches (25.5, 27, 27, 28 cm).

Shape underarm: BO 3 (3, 4, 4) sts at beginning of next two rows.

Continue in St st until work measures 16 (17, 17, 18) inches (40.5, 43, 43, 46 cm) from beginning.

Begin neck shaping: With right side facing, knit 20 (22, 22, 24) sts.

Put center 18 (18, 18, 18) sts on holder and remaining 20 (22, 22, 24) sts on another holder.

Decrease 1 st at neck edge every alternate row until 18 (19, 21, 22) sts remain.

Continue knitting until the piece measures 19 (20, 20, 21) inches (48.5, 51, 51, 53.5 cm).

BO sts.

Rejoin yarn to second set of shoulder sts.

Complete to match first half.

SLEEVES

With smaller needles and contrast yarn cast on 38 (38, 42, 44) sts and work 6 rows St st.

Color options

Change to main color and larger needles.

Increase 1 st on each side every 4 rows until there are 58 (62, 62, 66) sts on the needles.

Continue knitting until the sleeve measures 14 (14, 15, 15) inches (35.5, 35.5, 38, 38 cm) or desired length. Note: These measurements will give you three-quarter length sleeves; refer to the measurements in the variation if you prefer full-length sleeves.

BO loosely.

FINISHING

Note: To reduce bulk when seaming, carefully separate the yarn and use fewer strands, or use a thinner yarn of matching color.

Join one shoulder seam.

Using circular needle and main color, pick up and knit approximately 74 sts around neck edge including the sts left on center back and center front neck.

Change to contrast color and work 8 rows in St st.

BO loosely.

Seam second shoulder.

Seam neck band edges.

Pin the sleeve into the armhole and stitch in place.

Sew up the rest of the sleeve.

Sew up the side seams.

Note: The contrast color edges will roll so that the wrong side of the work shows on the right side. Take care to seam these edges appropriately.

Variation

This design is easily adapted to a longer version, with a full length sleeve. The version shown here was knit in a 100% wool yarn and the body was lengthened by 5 inches (12.5 cm).

MATERIALS

12 (13, 13, 14) balls in the main color (MC) and 2 balls in the contrast color (CC) of Lang's Polar 100% wool (55 m = 50 g) distributed by Berroco

For the longer sleeve cast on 32 (32, 36, 38) sts and continue to knit the sleeve as given in the pattern until there are 58 (62, 62, 66) sts on the needle and the sleeve measures 16 (16, 17, 17) inches or the desired length.

For the longer body, continue to knit rows until you are happy with the length.

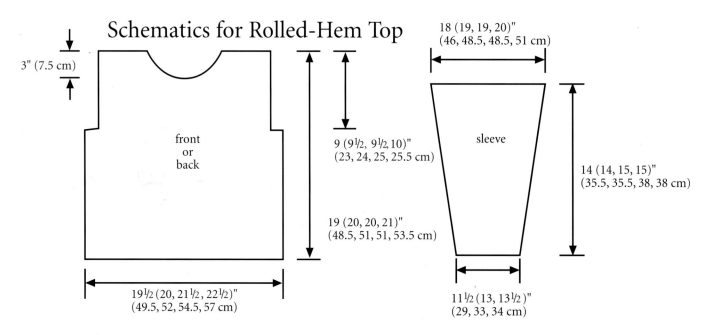

Schematics for Rolled-Hem Top

3" (7.5 cm)

front
or
back

9 (9½, 9½, 10)"
(23, 24, 25, 25.5 cm)

19 (20, 20, 21)"
(48.5, 51, 51, 53.5 cm)

19½ (20, 21½, 22½)"
(49.5, 52, 54.5, 57 cm)

18 (19, 19, 20)"
(46, 48.5, 48.5, 51 cm)

sleeve

14 (14, 15, 15)"
(35.5, 35.5, 38, 38 cm)

11½ (13, 13½)"
(29, 33, 34 cm)

Super Easy Tank Top

This zingy little summer special is cropped short for comfort, although you can easily add length if you prefer. The back and front are identical up to the shoulder area, then the back shoulder is extended so that it flaps over the front and is sewn in place. The buttons are purely decorative, so there aren't any buttonholes to worry about.

SIZES
Small (medium, large)

FINISHED MEASUREMENTS
Bust: 34 (38, 42) inches (86.5, 96.5, 107 cm)

Length: 14 (14½, 15) inches (35.5, 37, 38 cm)

MATERIALS
4 (5, 6) skeins (1 skein = 50 g, 154 yds/141 m) of Classic Elite's Atmosphere (100% cotton). Note: Yarn is used doubled.

Knitting needles in size 8 (5.0 mm) or size needed to obtain gauge

Decorative buttons

GAUGE
15 sts = 4 inches (10 cm) over garter st using two strands of yarn held together

FRONT
Holding two strands of yarn together, cast on 66 (74, 82) sts and work in garter st until the piece measures 7 (7, 7) inches (18, 18, 18 cm).

Shape armholes: BO 4 sts at beg of next 2 rows, 3 sts at beg of next 2 rows, 2 sts at beg of next 2 rows, 1 st at beg of next 2 rows. The number of sts remaining is 46 (54, 62).

When the piece measures 11 (11, 11) inches (28, 28, 28 cm), shape neck as follows: Knit 8 (10, 12) sts.

Place remaining sts on a holder and knit a further 3 (3½, 4) inches (7.5, 9, 10 cm).

BO the sts.

Rejoin yarn to sts on holder and BO the center 30 (34, 38) sts; working on the remaining 8 (10, 12) sts, complete to match the first side.

Novelty yarns add textural interest so that even the newest knitter can produce an eye-catching garment quite easily in basic stockinette or garter stitch. Small amounts of these yarns are also very effective when used as highlights in knitted pieces.

BACK

Work as given for the front, but knit the shoulder pieces to a total length of 7 (7½, 8) inches (18, 19, 20.5 cm).

FINISHING

Join side seams.

Fold the back shoulder extensions over onto front, and sew in place.

Attach buttons. Note: If you tie the buttons on they can be changed at your whim, or you can use decorative pins instead of buttons.

Schematic for Tank Top

7 (7½, 8)" (18, 19, 20 cm)

3 (3½, 4)" (7.5, 9, 10 cm)

4 (4, 4)" (10 cm)

front or back

7 (7, 7)" (18 cm)

11 (11, 11)" (28, 28, 28 cm)

17½ (19, 21½)" (44.5, 48.5, 54.5 cm)

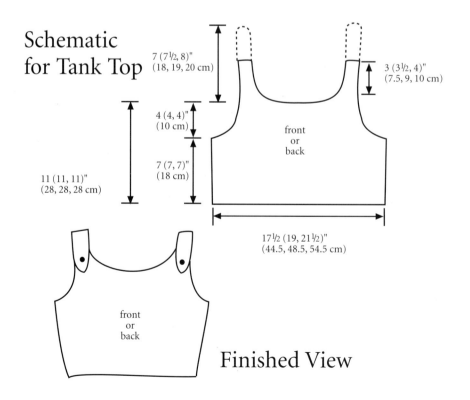

front or back

Finished View

Easy Flap-Front Top

This versatile top is unbelievably simple to make and offers a surprising number of wearing options. You can wear it with the flap open, highlighted by a pin or button, or with the flap closed. Or you can wear it the other way around: demure in front, vampish in back. And for those of you with the figure—lucky things—leave part of the side seams undone (see sketch) and ooh la la! This top is so quick and so very easy that you'll want to make several.

SIZES
Small (medium, large, extra large)

FINISHED MEASUREMENTS
Bust: 35 (38, 42, 44) inches (89, 96.5, 107, 112 cm)
Length: 16 (16½, 17, 17½) inches (40.5, 42, 43, 44.5 cm)

MATERIALS
6 (7, 7, 8) skeins of Classic Elite's 100% cotton Atmosphere (1 skein = 50 g [154 yds/141 m]). Note: Yarn used is doubled.
Knitting needles in size 9 (5.5 mm) or size needed to obtain gauge
Buttons as desired

GAUGE
15 sts = 4 inches (10 cm) over garter stitch, using 2 strands of yarn held together.
Note: Cast on the pieces loosely, using a larger needle for the cast-on row if necessary.

BACK
Holding two strands of yarn together, cast on 66 (72, 78, 82) sts and work in garter st (every row knit) until the piece measures 15 (15½, 16, 16½) inches (38, 39.5, 40.5, 42 cm).

Knit 20 (22, 24, 26) sts.

Leave these sts on a holder.

Cast off the center 26 (28, 30, 30) sts and knit across the remaining 20 (22, 24, 26) sts.

Knit 8 more rows (four garter stitch ridges).

BO the shoulder sts.

Return to sts on the holder and complete to match.

FRONT

Holding two strands of yarn together, cast on 66 (72, 78, 82) sts and work in garter st (every row knit) until the piece measures 10 (10½, 11, 11½) inches (25.5, 27, 28, 29 cm).

Next row, right side facing, knit 20 (22, 24, 26) sts, leaving the remaining sts on a holder.

Working on these sts only, knit until the piece measures the same as the back to shoulder.

BO (an easy way to make sure your measurements are the same is to count the number of garter stitch ridges on each piece).

Return to sts on the holder. Knit until piece measures 15 (15½, 16, 16½) inches (38, 39.5, 40.5, 42 cm).

BO 26 (28, 30, 30) sts and working on the remaining 20 (22, 24, 26) sts. Knit 8 more rows.

BO the sts.

FINISHING

Place markers on front and back 8 (8, 8½, 9) inches (20.5, 21.5, 23 cm) from start of shoulder shaping.

Join shoulder seams.

Join side seams below the markers.

Have fun deciding how you are going to trim the little top. You can leave it just as it is, of course, or choose one of the options presented here. If you have a stunning button, consider securing it with a strong matching or contrasting thread or thin leather cord. This becomes a feature in itself but also means the look can quickly be changed by untying the cord. A button can be stitched to one side of the opening and secured by a loop on the other side. Only one decision left now . . . which way 'round will you wear it?

Flap Top Options

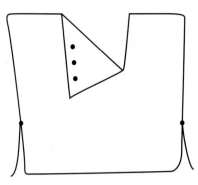

Sides seams can be left partially open and finished with a button.

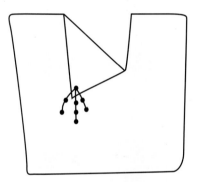

Flap can be embellished with buttons or beads

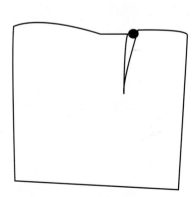

Flap can be worn closed with or without side vents.

Schematics for Easy Flap-Front Top

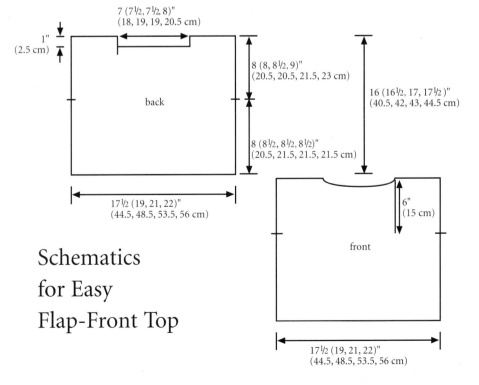

7 (7½, 7½, 8)"
(18, 19, 19, 20.5 cm)

1"
(2.5 cm)

back

8 (8, 8½, 9)"
(20.5, 20.5, 21.5, 23 cm)

16 (16½, 17, 17½)"
(40.5, 42, 43, 44.5 cm)

8 (8½, 8½, 8½)"
(20.5, 21.5, 21.5, 21.5 cm)

17½ (19, 21, 22)"
(44.5, 48.5, 53.5, 56 cm)

front

6"
(15 cm)

17½ (19, 21, 22)"
(44.5, 48.5, 53.5, 56 cm)

Pointed Hem Top

This top is formed by knitting individual triangles in garter stitch and then joining them together. Once all the triangles have been joined, both sides are identical and either side can be worn to the front. You can adjust the size and number of the triangles any way you like, as long as you have the correct number of total stitches. This top is an ideal candidate for embellishment. (See pages 115-122 for ideas and inspiration.)

SIZES
Small (medium, large)

FINISHED MEASUREMENTS
Bust: 36 (40, 44) inches (91.5, 101.5, 112 cm)

MATERIALS
5 (6, 7) skeins (1 skein = 50 g, 98 yds/90 m) Berroco's Sprite (35% cotton, 35% rayon, 30% nylon)

Needles in size 7 (4.5 mm) or in size to obtain gauge

Embellishments of choice

GAUGE
20 sts = 5 inches (13 cm) (4 sts = 1 inch [2.5 cm]) measured over garter st

PATTERN STITCH
Garter st = every row knit

*Note: The back and front are identical once all of the triangles have been joined. One piece has three triangles and the other has four, and either side can be worn to the front. You can adjust the size and number of triangles any way you like, just be sure you have the correct number of stitches in total.

TO MAKE A TRIANGLE:
Cast on 2 sts.

Knit one row.

Increase 1 st at the beg of the next and every row to the required number of stitches.

Leave the stitches on a holder.

FIRST PART
Make a total of three triangles for each size, using the number of stitches indicated for each triangle in your size category.

Small (20, 24, 28) stitches = total of 72 stitches

Medium (23, 27, 30) stitches = total of 80 stitches

Large (26, 30, 32) stitches = total of 88 stitches

When you have completed the triangles, arrange them on the needle in the order most pleasing to you and knit across all the stitches.

Continue in garter st until the piece measures about 16 inches (40.5 cm) at the side seam.

Knit 22 (24, 26) sts.

Leave remaining sts on a holder and work on these sts for 2 inches (5 cm).

BO.

Rejoin yarn to the sts on the holder.

BO 28 (32, 36) sts and work on the remaining 22 (24, 26) sts to match the first shoulder.

BO.

SECOND PART

Make a total of four triangles for each size, using the number of stitches indicated for each triangle in your size category.

Size (1st, 2nd, 3rd, 4th triangle)

Small (15, 18, 18, 21) stitches = total of 72 stitches.

Medium (17, 20, 20, 23) stitches = total of 80 stitches.

Large (18, 21, 23, 26) stitches = total of 88 stitches.

When all the triangles are completed, continue as given for the first part.

FINISHING

Place markers 8 (8½, 9) inches (20.5, 21.5, 23 cm) from top of shoulder.

Join shoulder seams.

Join side seams below markers.

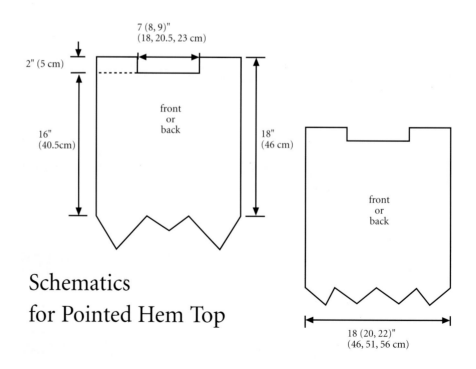

7 (8, 9)"
(18, 20.5, 23 cm)

2" (5 cm)

16"
(40.5cm)

front
or
back

18"
(46 cm)

front
or
back

18 (20, 22)"
(46, 51, 56 cm)

Schematics
for Pointed Hem Top

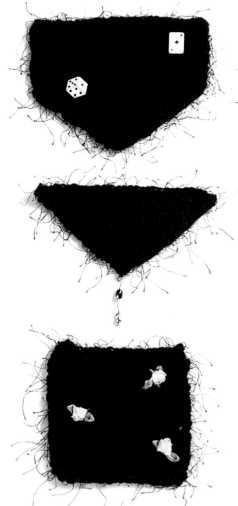

Embellishing the points with strands of beads and using a textured yarn creates a totally different look with same pattern.

Above: For a classic black top, choose a soft, drapey yarn with a little textural interest so that the finished top will make a statement all its own when worn perfectly plain.

Below: For an ethnic look, a soft cotton yarn with texture and occasional color highlights creates a knitted fabric particularly suited to leather, wood, or bone attachments.

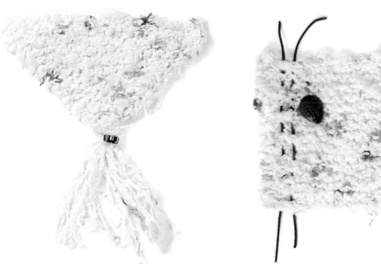

Great Tunics

Loose, comfortable tunics are simple to wear and easy to knit. Several variations are shown here. Each offers something special, although the body and sleeves are the same for each. The blue tunic has an interesting rib variation which doesn't hug the hips. Its color theme—subtle variations of blue—looks great with denim. The grey tunic is a useful little number, working well as relaxed weekend wear or as a striking topper for a pair of well-cut dressy pants. The mauve tunic features a slightly more fitted shape because of the wide rib stitch hems. Additional tunic options are limited only by your imagination and enthusiasm.

VIEW 1. The Blue Tunic

VIEW 2. The Charcoal / Gray Tunic

VIEW 3. The Mauve Tunic

SIZES
Petite (small, medium, large, extra large)

FINISHED MEASUREMENTS
Bust: 39 (41, 43, 45, 47) inches (99, 104, 109, 114.5, 119.5 cm)

Length: 28 (28½, 29, 30, 30½) inches (71, 72.5, 74, 76, 77.5 cm)

Sleeve length: 18 (18½, 18½, 19, 19) inches (46, 47, 47, 48.5, 48.5 cm)

MATERIALS
Plymouth Yarn Company's Encore worsted weight yarn (75% acrylic, 25% wool)

View 1 (blue): 6 (7, 7, 7, 8) balls

View 2 (gray): 6 (6, 7, 7, 7) balls MC, 1 (1, 1, 1, 1) ball contrast

Decorative buttons (optional)

View 3 (mauve): 6 (7, 7, 7, 8) balls

Knitting needles in sizes 9 and 7 (5.5 mm and 4.5 mm) or size to obtain gauge

GAUGE
18 sts and 24 rows = 4 inches (10 cm) measured over

St st with larger needles

BACK
View 1. Using smaller needles, cast on 88 (92, 98, 102, 106) sts and knit three rows. Right side facing: row 1 knit to end; row 2 K1P1 to end of row. Repeat these two rows 6 times more. Knit 4 rows. Right side facing, change to larger needles and continue in St st.

View 2. Using smaller needles and contrast color, cast on 88 (92, 98, 102, 106) sts and work 3 ins (7.5 cm) in St st. Change to larger needles, and continue in St st until work measures 5 inches (12.5 cm). Change to MC and continue as given for View 1.

View 3. With smaller needles, cast on 86 (90, 98, 102, 106) sts. 1st row: K1(K3P1) to the last st, P1. Continue in K3P1 rib as established for 2 inches (5 cm). Change to larger needles and St st, increasing 1 st at each side for first and second sizes only. 88 (92, 98, 102, 106) sts. Continue as for View 1.

For all views: Continue in St st until work measures 16 (16½, 16½, 17, 17) inches (40.5, 42, 42, 43, 43 cm) or desired length.

Shape underarm: BO 4 (4, 5, 7, 7) sts at beg of next two rows.

When work measures 26½ (27, 27½, 28½, 29) inches (67.5, 68.5, 70, 72.5, 74 cm) shape back neck: with right side facing, knit 28 (30, 31, 31, 32) sts. Place rest of sts on holder. Decrease 1 st at neck edge on next and every alternate row, 3 times. Knit until work measures 28

(28½, 29, 30, 30½) inches (71, 72.5, 74, 76, 77.5 cm). BO the 25 (27, 28, 28, 29) shoulder sts. Return to sts on holder. Knit across 24 (24, 26, 26, 28) sts and place these on holder for center back neck. Continue on remaining sts and work to correspond with the first side.

FRONT

Work as given for back until the work measures 25 (25½, 26, 27, 27½) inches (63.5, 64.8, 66, 68.5, 70 cm).

Begin neck shaping: With right side facing, knit 31 (33, 35, 35, 35) sts and place rest of sts on a holder. Decrease 1 st at neck edge every alternate row until 25 (27, 28, 28, 29) sts remain.

Work straight until the piece measures the same as the back.

BO the shoulder sts.

Return to the sts on the holder, leave center 18 (18, 18, 18, 22) sts on holder, rejoin yarn to the remaining sts and work decreases at neck edge as before. Complete to match the first side.

SLEEVE

View 1: Using smaller needles, cast on 38 (40, 44, 44, 46) sts. Work 3 inches (7.5 cm) in the rib pattern as given for back.

View 2: Using smaller needles, cast on 38 (40, 44, 44, 46) sts and knit 1 inch (2.5 cm) in St st, change to larger needles and work 2 more inches (5 cm) in St st.

Close-up views of rolled hem and button embellishment options

Close-up view of hem variations

View 3: Using smaller needles, cast on 38 (42, 46, 46, 46) sts. Work in the rib pattern for 3 inches (7.5 cm).

All views: With larger needles, continue knitting in St st, increasing 1 st on each side of the next row and every following 3rd row until there are 86 (86, 90, 94, 100) sts.

Continue knitting until sleeve measures 18 (18½, 18½, 19, 19) inches (46, 47, 47, 48.5, 48.5 cm).

BO loosely.

FINISHING

All views: Seam one shoulder together.

Neckband: Using smaller needles, with right side facing, pick up and knit approx 84 (86, 88, 90, 92) sts around neck edge, including sts left on holders. Check that you have picked up sts evenly.

Views 1 and 3: Knit 8 rows (you will have 4 garter st ridges). BO loosely.

View 2: Work 1½ inches (4 cm) in St st. BO loosely.

All views: Seam shoulder and neck band edges neatly.

Sew sleeves in place between markers.

Sew up side and sleeve seams, taking care to match seams at sleeve and hem bands.

View 2: Add decorative buttons if desired.

Schematics for Tunics

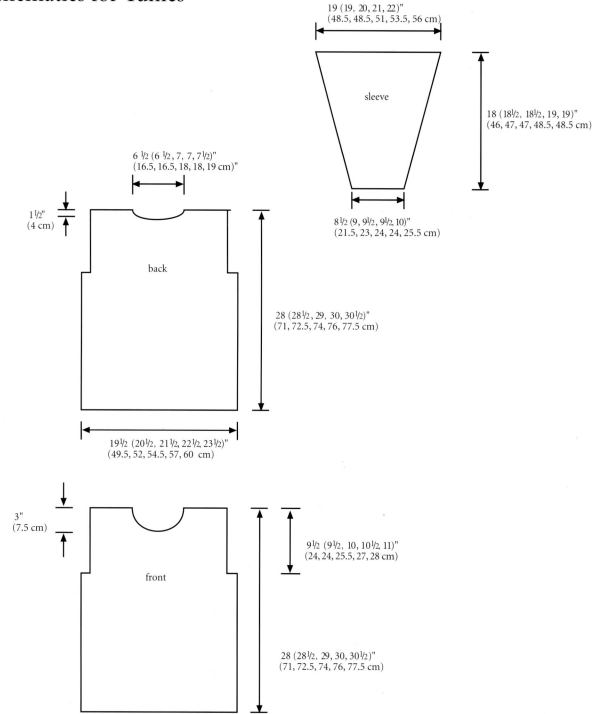

19 (19, 20, 21, 22)"
(48.5, 48.5, 51, 53.5, 56 cm)

sleeve

18 (18½, 18½, 19, 19)"
(46, 47, 47, 48.5, 48.5 cm)

8½ (9, 9½, 9½, 10)"
(21.5, 23, 24, 24, 25.5 cm)

6 ½ (6 ½, 7, 7, 7½)"
(16.5, 16.5, 18, 18, 19 cm)"

1½"
(4 cm)

back

28 (28½, 29, 30, 30½)"
(71, 72.5, 74, 76, 77.5 cm)

19½ (20½, 21½, 22½, 23½)"
(49.5, 52, 54.5, 57, 60 cm)

3"
(7.5 cm)

front

9½ (9½, 10, 10½, 11)"
(24, 24, 25.5, 27, 28 cm)

28 (28½, 29, 30, 30½)"
(71, 72.5, 74, 76, 77.5 cm)

A NOTE ABOUT CHILDREN'S SIZES:
Because children of the same age come in so many different shapes and sizes, I have given sizes based on finished chest measurements instead of by age. Choose which size to knit based on the intended wearer's chest measurement, taking care to make the fit generous enough to provide freedom of movement. The body and sleeves of the garment can be lengthened if necessary, just allow extra yarn.

CHILDREN'S
SWEATERS

I loved knitting for my daughters when they were little. The brighter and simpler, the better I liked it. Color blocking is quick and easy for knitters of all levels, while a few striking buttons ensure cheerful results. Before long, you'll have a stash of yarn oddments, leading to even more happy sweaters. So mix and match, let your favorite little ones choose colors, and have the greatest fun!

Color-Blocked Jacket with Choice of Detachable Hoods

These fun jackets are color-blocked with contrasting colors of yarn for the ribbing and body pieces. Two styles of hoods are shown, both of which button on and off. The buttons serve as decorative trim when the hoods are off.

FINISHED MEASUREMENTS
Chest: approximately 25 (26, 27, 28, 30) inches (63.5, 66, 68.6, 71, 76 cm)

MATERIALS
Plymouth Yarn Company's Encore worsted weight yarn, 75% acrylic 25% wool in an assortment of colors that total about 300 (325, 350, 375, 400) grams

Knitting needles in size 8 and 6 (5.0 and 4.0 mm) or size needed to obtain correct gauge

Buttons for front closure

5 buttons for bobble hood or decorative buttons for the school hood

GAUGE
20 sts = 4 inches (10 cm) in St st on larger needles

BACK
Using smaller needles, cast on 62 (66, 68, 72, 76) sts.

Work 1½ (1½, 2, 2, 2) inches (4, 4, 5, 5, 5 cm) in K1P1 rib.

Change to larger needles and work in St st until back measures 12 (13, 14, 15, 16) inches (30.5, 33, 35.5, 38, 40.5 cm).

BO 20 (22, 22, 22, 24) sts on each side for the shoulders.

Leave remaining 22 (22, 24, 28, 28) sts on holder for back neck.

Place markers for underarm 5 (5½, 6, 6½, 7) inches (13, 14, 15, 16.5, 18 cm) from top of shoulder.

LEFT FRONT
With smaller needles, cast on 31 (33, 34, 36, 38) sts and work in rib as for back.

Change to larger needles and work in St st until front measures 9½ (10½, 11½, 12½, 13) inches (24, 27, 29, 32, 33 cm).

Begin neck shaping: At neck edge BO 8 (8, 8, 10, 10) sts, then decrease 1 st at neck edge every alternate row until 20 (22, 22, 22, 24) sts remain.

Work straight until front measures the same as the back.

BO all sts.

RIGHT FRONT
Work same as left front, reversing all shaping.

Place markers on the fronts for underarm.

SLEEVES
Using smaller needles, cast on 32 (32, 36, 38, 40) sts and work in K1P1 rib for 1½ (1½, 2, 2, 2) inches (4, 4, 5, 5, 5 cm).

Change to larger needles and knit in St st, increasing 1 st each side every 4 rows until there are 50 (56, 60, 66, 70) sts on the needle.

Continue working until sleeve measures 8 (9, 10, 11, 12) inches (20.5, 23, 25.5, 28, 30.5 cm).

BO all sts.

NECK BAND
Sew shoulder seams tog.

With right side facing, smaller needles and color of choice, pick up and knit approximately 60 (62, 70, 74, 80) sts around neck edge, including sts on holder.

Rib for 8 rows.

BO sts in rib.

BUTTON BAND

With smaller needles and color of choice and with right side facing, pick up and knit approximately 42 (46, 50, 54, 56) sts along left front edge from top of neck band to bottom edge of ribbing.

Rib for 8 rows.

BO sts in rib.

Sew on 5 or 6 buttons, spacing evenly.

BUTTONHOLE BAND

Pick up sts as for button band.

Work buttonholes in 5th row to correspond with buttons.

Rib 3 more rows and BO sts in rib.

Check that your bands lie flat and that the sts are picked up evenly. (See pages 19 and 20 for suggestions and tips on this technique.)

FINISHING

Sew 5 buttons in middle of neckband, placing them as follows:

One at center back, one at each shoulder seam, and one each at first neck shaping decrease.

Sew sleeves in place between markers.

Sew side and sleeve seams.

BOBBLE HOOD (2 SIZES GIVEN)

Using smaller needles and color of choice, cast on 35 sts for both sizes.

Work 4 rows rib.

Make 3 buttonholes in next row as follows:

Rib 3, yfd k2tog, rib 12, yfd k2tog, rib 11, yfd k2tog, rib 3.

Work 3 more rows in rib.

Next row: increase in every stitch = 70 sts.

Change to larger needles and 2nd color.

Continue in St st until work measures 7 (8) inches (18, 20.5 cm) from cast-on edge.

Bobble hood

With right side facing, cast off 20 sts, work to end of row.

Cast off 20 sts and work to end.

Continue knitting on remaining sts until center piece fits along bound-off edges.

BO all sts.

Sew center piece to bound-off edges.

Using smaller needles and color of choice, pick up and knit approximately 90 (100) sts along front edge of hood.

Work 6 rows in rib.

Next row: make 2 more buttonholes as follows:

Rib 5, yfd k2tog, rib to last 7 sts, yfd k2tog, rib to end.

Work 3 more rows.

BO all sts.

BOBBLES
Make as follows:

Cast on 1 st, leaving a length of yarn to secure bobble with, then k1, p1, k1, p1 into the st (total of 5 sts).

Work 4 rows St st. Cut yarn, thread tightly through sts.

Thread the tails into a tapestry needle and knot the bobbles to the hood in desired positions.

SCHOOL HOOD
Work as for basic hood, casting on with red yarn for ribbing.

Work St st in 3 rows white, 1 row black until center panel sts remain (30 sts).

Continue in black.

Work face ribbing in green.

Decorate with school theme buttons as desired.

Button hood onto sweater.

School hood

Schematics for Color-Blocked Jacket With Detachable Hoods

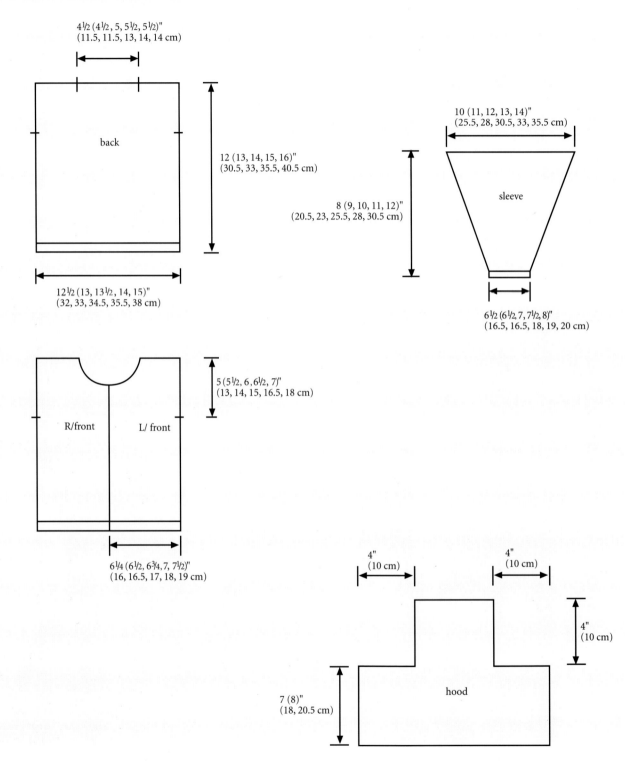

$4\frac{1}{2}$ ($4\frac{1}{2}$, 5, $5\frac{1}{2}$, $5\frac{1}{2}$)"
(11.5, 11.5, 13, 14, 14 cm)

back

12 (13, 14, 15, 16)"
(30.5, 33, 35.5, 40.5 cm)

$12\frac{1}{2}$ (13, $13\frac{1}{2}$, 14, 15)"
(32, 33, 34.5, 35.5, 38 cm)

10 (11, 12, 13, 14)"
(25.5, 28, 30.5, 33, 35.5 cm)

sleeve

8 (9, 10, 11, 12)"
(20.5, 23, 25.5, 28, 30.5 cm)

$6\frac{1}{2}$ ($6\frac{1}{2}$, 7, $7\frac{1}{2}$, 8)"
(16.5, 16.5, 18, 19, 20 cm)

R/front   L/ front

5 ($5\frac{1}{2}$, 6, $6\frac{1}{2}$, 7)"
(13, 14, 15, 16.5, 18 cm)

$6\frac{1}{4}$ ($6\frac{1}{2}$, $6\frac{3}{4}$, 7, $7\frac{1}{2}$)"
(16, 16.5, 17, 18, 19 cm)

4"
(10 cm)

4"
(10 cm)

4"
(10 cm)

hood

7 (8)"
(18, 20.5 cm)

V-Neck Cardigan

The simple ridged pattern stitch in this sweater makes a great frame for buttons or bobbles. You can knit the ridges in the same color as the sweater, in a contrasting color, or in any combination you like.

FINISHED MEASUREMENTS
Chest: approximately 25 (26, 27, 28, 30) inches (63.5, 66, 68.5, 71, 76 cm)

MATERIALS
2 (2, 3, 3, 3) 100 g balls Plymouth Yarn Company's Encore worsted weight yarn (75% acrylic, 25% wool)

Knitting needles in size 8 and 6 (5.0 and 4.0 mm) or size needed to obtain correct gauge

Circular needle in size 6 (4.0 mm)

5 buttons for front closure

GAUGE
20 sts = 4 inches (10 cm) measured over St st with larger needles

PATTERN STITCH
Rows 1 – 7 in St st

Row 8 (wrong side facing) knit

BACK
Using smaller needles, cast on 62 (66, 68, 72, 76) sts.

Work 1½ (1½, 2, 2, 2) inches (4, 4, 5, 5, 5 cm) in K1P1 rib.

Change to larger needles and work in pattern stitch as given until back measures 11 (12, 13, 14, 15) inches (28, 30.5, 33, 35.5, 38 cm).

BO 20 (22, 22, 22, 24) sts on each side for the shoulders.

Leave remaining 22 (22, 24, 28, 28) sts on holder for back neck.

Place markers for underarm 5 (5½, 6, 6½, 7) inches (13, 14, 15, 16.5, 18 cm) from top of shoulder.

LEFT FRONT
With smaller needles, cast on 31 (33, 34, 36, 38) sts and work in rib as for back.

Change to larger needles and work in pattern st until front measures same as back to underarm.

Continuing in pattern stitch, begin neck shaping: right side facing knit to last 3 sts, K2 tog, K1.

Continue to decrease 1 st at neck edge every 2 rows until 20 (22, 22, 22, 24) sts remain.

Continue to knit until front matches back to shoulder.

RIGHT FRONT
Work same as left front, reversing all shaping.

SLEEVES
Using smaller needles, cast on 32 (32, 36, 38, 40) sts and work in K1P1 rib for 1½ (1½, 2, 2, 2) inches (4, 4, 5, 5, 5 cm).

Change to larger needles and work in pattern st, increasing 1 st each side every 4 rows until there are 50 (56, 60, 66, 70) sts on the needle.

Continue working until sleeve measures 8 (9, 10, 11, 12) inches (20.5, 23, 25.5, 28, 30.5 cm).

BO all sts.

NECK BANDS
Mark position of buttons on left front, the first to come 1/2 inch (1.5 cm) from cast-on edge and the last 1/2 inch (1.5 cm) below start of neck shaping.

Using circular needle, pick up and knit approximately 46 (52, 56, 60, 64) sts along right front edge, 22 (22, 24, 28, 28) across back neck, and then approximately 46 (52, 56, 60, 64) along left

front edge. This is a total of approximately 114 (126, 136, 148, 156) sts.

Next row, with right sides facing, make buttonholes to correspond to markers on left front.

Work 3 more rows.

BO in rib.

Note: If making garment for a boy, reverse position of buttons and buttonholes.

FINISHING

Stitch shoulder seams together.

Sew tops of sleeves in place between markers.

Join sleeve and side seams.

Sew on buttons to correspond with buttonholes.

Embellish as desired with buttons.

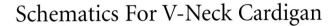

Schematics For V-Neck Cardigan

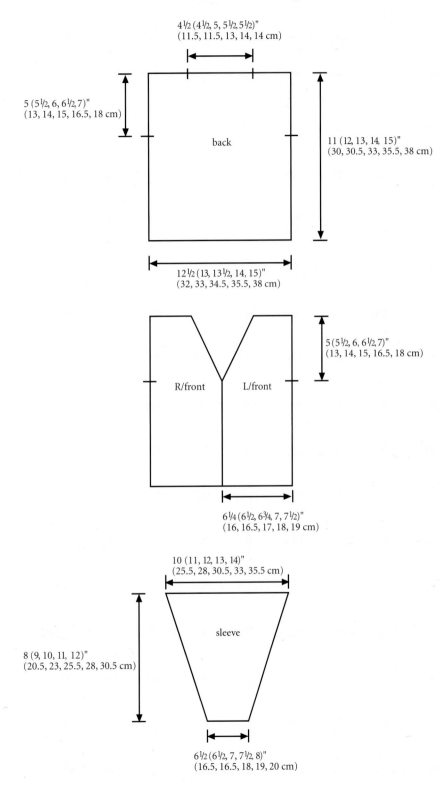

4½ (4½, 5, 5½, 5½)"
(11.5, 11.5, 13, 14, 14 cm)

5 (5½, 6, 6½, 7)"
(13, 14, 15, 16.5, 18 cm)

back

11 (12, 13, 14, 15)"
(30, 30.5, 33, 35.5, 38 cm)

12½ (13, 13½, 14, 15)"
(32, 33, 34.5, 35.5, 38 cm)

R/front   L/front

5 (5½, 6, 6½, 7)"
(13, 14, 15, 16.5, 18 cm)

6¼ (6½, 6¾, 7, 7½)"
(16, 16.5, 17, 18, 19 cm)

10 (11, 12, 13, 14)"
(25.5, 28, 30.5, 33, 35.5 cm)

sleeve

8 (9, 10, 11, 12)"
(20.5, 23, 25.5, 28, 30.5 cm)

6½ (6½, 7, 7½, 8)"
(16.5, 16.5, 18, 19, 20 cm)

Short Sleeve Crew-Neck Sweater

Star buttons make a fun trim for this cute sweater. The short sleeves work well as part of a twin set under the cardigan on page 101.

FINISHED MEASUREMENTS

Chest: approximately 25 (26, 27, 28, 30) inches (63.5, 66, 68.5, 71, 76 cm)

MATERIALS

2 (2, 2, 3, 3) 100 g balls Plymouth Yarn Company's Encore worsted weight yarn (75% acrylic, 25% wool)

Knitting needles in sizes 8 and 6 (5.0 and 4.0 mm) or size needed to obtain correct gauge

Decorative buttons

GAUGE

20 sts = 4 inches (10 cm) measured over St st with larger needles

BACK

Using smaller needles, cast on 62 (66, 68, 72, 76) sts and work 1½ (1½, 2, 2, 2) inches (4, 4, 5, 5, 5 cm) in K1P1 rib.

Change to larger needles and work in St st until back measures 11 (12, 13, 14, 15) inches (28, 30.5, 33, 35.5, 38 cm).

BO 20 (22, 22, 22, 24) sts on each side for the shoulders.

Leave remaining 22 (22, 24, 28, 28) sts on holder for back neck.

Place markers for underarm 5 (5½, 6, 6½, 7) inches (13, 14, 15, 16.5, 18 cm) from top of shoulder.

FRONT

Work as given for back until the piece measures 8½ (9½, 10½, 11, 12) inches (21.5, 24, 27, 28, 30.5 cm).

Begin neck shaping: With right sides facing, knit 23 (25, 26, 26, 28) sts.

Place the remaining sts on a holder.

Decrease 1 st at neck edge, working the decreases 1 st in from the edge, on every alternate row until 20 (22, 22, 22, 24) sts remain.

Continue until the work measures the same as back to the shoulder.

BO shoulder sts.

Return to the sts on the holder, leaving the center 16 (16, 16, 20, 20) sts on holder and knit across the remaining sts.

Complete neck shaping to match the other side, reversing all shapings.

BO shoulder sts.

SLEEVES

Using smaller needles, cast on 40 (46, 50, 56, 60) sts and work in K1P1 rib for 1 (1, 1, 1½, 1½) inches (2.5, 2.5, 2.5, 4, 4 cm).

Change to larger needles and work in St st, increasing 10 sts evenly across the first row for all sizes. You should have 50 (56, 60, 66, 70) sts.

Knit until sleeve measures 4 (4, 4½, 4½, 5) inches (10, 10, 11.5, 11.5, 13 cm) from beginning.

BO all sts.

NECK BAND

Seam one shoulder.

With smaller needle, pick up and knit approx 62 (68, 74, 76, 80) sts.

Work in rib for about 1 inch (2.5 cm).

BO the sts.

FINISHING

Stitch shoulder and neck band seam.

Sew tops of sleeves in place between markers.

Join sleeve and side seams.

Embellish as desired.

Schematics for Short Sleeve Crew-Neck Sweater

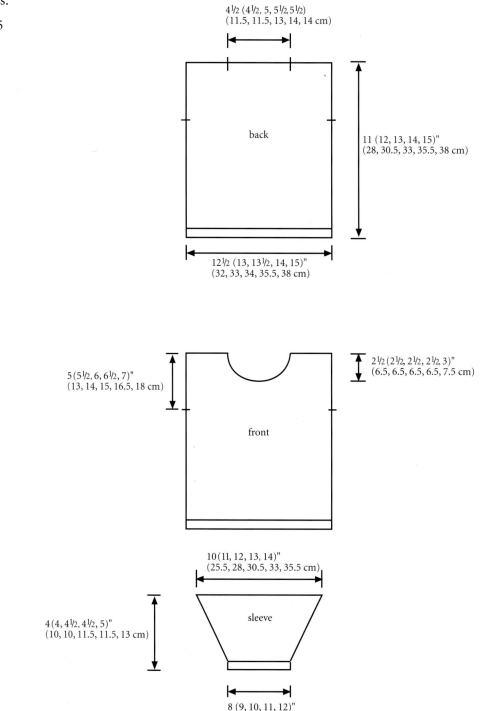

4½ (4½, 5, 5½, 5½)
(11.5, 11.5, 13, 14, 14 cm)

back

11 (12, 13, 14, 15)"
(28, 30.5, 33, 35.5, 38 cm)

12½ (13, 13½, 14, 15)"
(32, 33, 34, 35.5, 38 cm)

5 (5½, 6, 6½, 7)"
(13, 14, 15, 16.5, 18 cm)

2½ (2½, 2½, 2½, 3)"
(6.5, 6.5, 6.5, 6.5, 7.5 cm)

front

10 (11, 12, 13, 14)"
(25.5, 28, 30.5, 33, 35.5 cm)

sleeve

4 (4, 4½, 4½, 5)"
(10, 10, 11.5, 11.5, 13 cm)

8 (9, 10, 11, 12)"
(20.5, 23, 25.5, 28, 30.5 cm)

Pointed Hem Vest

This vest shape looks great on boys and girls and really grows with the child. The points make a nice on-the-go project. Each one takes only a few minutes to knit so you'll soon have a bag of them.

FINISHED MEASUREMENTS

Chest: approximately 24 (26, 28, 30) inches (61, 66, 71, 76 cm)

MATERIALS

2 (3, 3, 3) balls in main color (MC) in Plymouth Yarn Company's Encore worsted weight yarn (75% acrylic, 25% wool) and small amounts of contrasting yarn in red, yellow, turquoise, and purple (or other colors of your choice)

Knitting needles in sizes 8 and 6 (5.0 and 4.0 mm) or size needed to obtain correct gauge

Circular needle in size 6 (4.0 mm)

4 buttons

GAUGE

20 sts = 4 inches (10 cm) measured over St st with larger needles

TO MAKE A TRIANGLE:

Cast on 2 sts, using larger needles. Knit 1 row. Inc 1 st at beg of every row to 12 (13, 14, 15) sts.

Leave the sts on a holder.

Make a total of ten knitted triangles.

BOTTOM BAND

Arrange the ten triangles on the needle.

Using red, knit across all the sts 120 (130, 140, 150) sts.

Knit the next row (1 garter st ridge).

With right side facing, join in yellow and work 6 rows in St st.

With red, knit the next two rows (1 garter st ridge).

DIVIDE STS FOR BACK & FRONTS:

With right side facing and MC, knit 30 (33, 35, 38) sts and place these on a holder for the right front.

Knit across the next 60 (64, 70, 74) sts for the back and place the remaining 30 (33, 35, 38) sts on a holder for the left front.

Working only on the sts for the back, increase 1 st at each end to form the seam allowance; you should have 62 (66, 72, 76) sts on the needle.

BACK

Knit in St st until work measures about 12 (13, 14, 15) inches (30.5, 33, 35.5, 38 cm).

BO 21 (23, 25, 26) sts on each side for shoulders and place remaining 20 (20, 22, 24) back neck sts on a holder.

Measure 5½ (6, 6, 6½) inches (14, 15, 15, 16.5 cm) down from the shoulder and place markers for the underarm.

LEFT FRONT

Replace sts on needle and work in St st in main color, increasing one st at the side seam edge until left front is the same length as back to underarm, ending with right side facing.

Begin neck shaping: Decrease 1 st at neck edge every 3 rows until 21 (23, 25, 26) sts remain.

Work until the piece measures the same as the back to the shoulder.

BO all sts.

Place markers as on back for underarm.

RIGHT FRONT

Work same as left front, reversing all shaping.

ARM BANDS

Sew shoulder seams together.

Using smaller needles and red yarn, with right side facing, pick up and knit approximately 50 (56, 56, 60) sts between the markers.

Knit 1 more row (1 garter st ridge).

Change to yellow and work in K1P1 rib for about 1 inch (2.5 cm).

BO all sts in rib.

FRONT BANDS

Mark position of buttons on left front, spacing them evenly (see photo).

Using circular needle and red yarn, pick up and knit approx 124 (134, 146, 154) sts evenly along the right front edge, across the back neck includng any sts on holder, and along the left front edge.

Knit the next row (1 garter st ridge).

Using turquoise, work 2 rows in K1P1 rib.

Next row, right side facing, make buttonholes to correspond to markers on left front.

Work 3 more rows.

BO in rib.

Note: If making garment for a boy, reverse position of buttons and buttonholes.

FINISHING

Stitch underarm and side seams.

Sew on buttons.

Schematics for Pointed Hem Vest

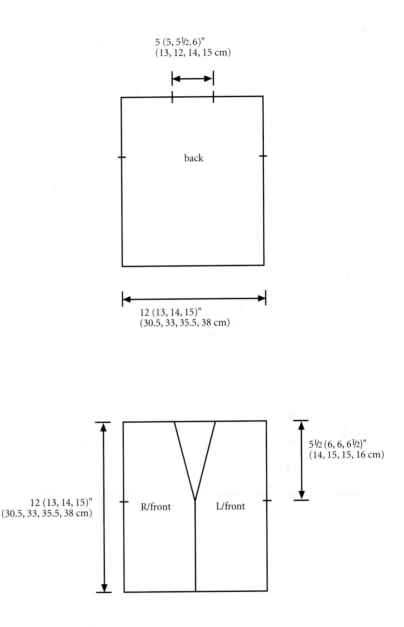

5 (5, 5½, 6)"
(13, 12, 14, 15 cm)

back

12 (13, 14, 15)"
(30.5, 33, 35.5, 38 cm)

5½ (6, 6, 6½)"
(14, 15, 15, 16 cm)

12 (13, 14, 15)"
(30.5, 33, 35.5, 38 cm)

R/front   L/front

Long Sleeve
Crew-Neck Sweater

The simple garter stitch ridge pattern in this sweater can be knit in the same color as the sweater or in a contrasting color as shown here. The contrasting color is also used for the cast-on edges.

FINISHED MEASUREMENTS

Chest: approximately 25 (26, 27, 28, 30) inches (63.5, 66, 68.5, 71, 76 cm)

MATERIALS

2 (3, 3, 3, 3) 100 g balls of main color (MC) in Plymouth Yarn Company's Encore worsted weight yarn (75% acrylic 25% wool)

Small amount of yarn in contrasting color

Knitting needles in sizes 8 and 6 (5.0 and 4.0 mm) or size needed to obtain correct gauge

Decorative buttons (optional)

GAUGE

20 sts = 4 inches (10 cm) measured over St st with larger needles

PATTERN STITCH

Rows 1 – 6 in St st

Rows 7 and 8: Knit using contrast color

BACK

Using smaller needles and contrast color, cast on 62 (66, 68, 72, 76) sts.

Change to main color and work 1½ (1½, 2, 2, 2) inches (4, 4, 5, 5, 5 cm) in K1P1 rib.

Change to larger needles and work in pattern stitch as given for a total of three repeats. Continue in main color and St st until back measures 11 (12, 13, 14, 15) inches (28, 30.5, 33, 35.5, 38 cm).

BO 20 (22, 22, 22, 24) sts on each side for the shoulders.

Leave remaining 22 (22, 24, 28, 28) sts on holder for back neck.

Place markers for underarm 5 (5½, 6, 6½, 7) inches (13, 14, 15, 16.5, 18 cm) from top of shoulder.

FRONT

Work as given for back until the piece measures 8½ (9½, 10½, 11, 12) inches (21.5, 24, 27, 28, 30.5 cm).

Begin neck shaping: With right side facing, knit 23 (25, 26, 26, 28) sts.

Place the remaining sts on a holder.

Decrease 1 st at neck edge, working the decreases 1 st in from the edge on every alternate row until 20 (22, 22, 22, 24) sts remain.

Continue until the work measures the same as back to the shoulder.

BO shoulder sts.

Return to the sts on the holder; leave the center 16 (16, 16, 20, 20) sts on holder and knit across the remaining sts.

Complete neck shaping to match the other side, reversing all shapings.

BO shoulder sts.

SLEEVES

Using smaller needles and contrast yarn, cast on 32 (32, 36, 38, 40) sts.

Change to MC and work in K1P1 rib for 1½ (1½, 2, 2, 2) inches (4, 4, 5, 5, 5 cm)

Change to larger needles and work in pattern st for a total of 2 repeats continuing in MC and St st, while increasing 1 st each side every 4 rows until there are 50 (56, 60, 66, 70) sts on the needle.

Continue working until sleeve measures 8 (9, 10, 11, 12) inches (20.5, 23, 25.4, 28, 30.5 cm).

BO all sts.

NECK BAND

Seam one shoulder.

With smaller needle and main color, pick up approximately 62 (68, 74, 76, 80) stitches all around neck edge, including those left on holders.

Work in rib for about 1 inch (2.5 cm).

BO the sts.

FINISHING

Stitch shoulder and neck band seam.

Sew tops of sleeves in place between markers.

Join sleeve and side seams.

Embellish as desired.

Schematics for
Long Sleeve Crew-Neck Sweater

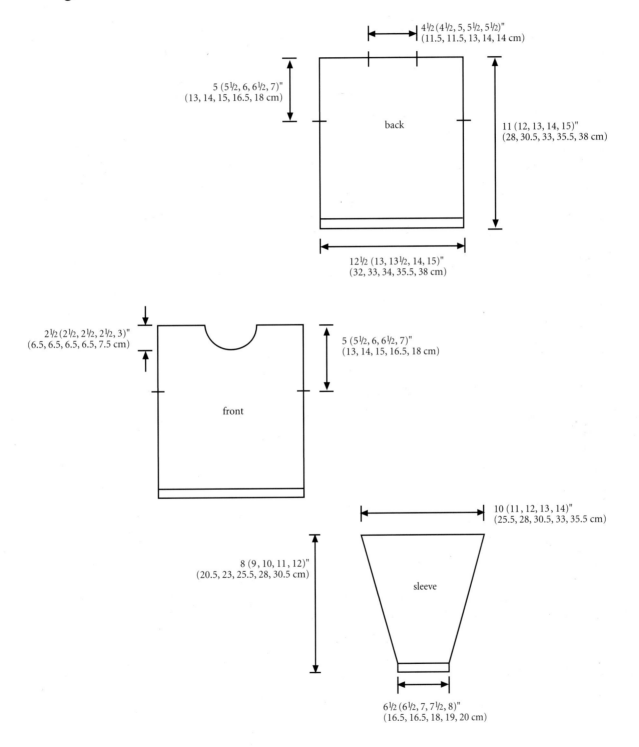

4½ (4½, 5, 5½, 5½)"
(11.5, 11.5, 13, 14, 14 cm)

5 (5½, 6, 6½, 7)"
(13, 14, 15, 16.5, 18 cm)

back

11 (12, 13, 14, 15)"
(28, 30.5, 33, 35.5, 38 cm)

12½ (13, 13½, 14, 15)"
(32, 33, 34, 35.5, 38 cm)

2½ (2½, 2½, 2½, 3)"
(6.5, 6.5, 6.5, 6.5, 7.5 cm)

5 (5½, 6, 6½, 7)"
(13, 14, 15, 16.5, 18 cm)

front

10 (11, 12, 13, 14)"
(25.5, 28, 30.5, 33, 35.5 cm)

8 (9, 10, 11, 12)"
(20.5, 23, 25.5, 28, 30.5 cm)

sleeve

6½ (6½, 7, 7½, 8)"
(16.5, 16.5, 18, 19, 20 cm)

EMBELLISHMENT

Embellishment can transform even the plainest garments. Much as I adore knitting, I confess to having 'cheated' by purchasing sweaters to which I have added my own touches. If you are going to do this, look for high quality knits available during sale periods and embellish them.

Celebrating the Unique

Detail is something which always sets the unique apart from the mass produced. Most commercial knits do not feature a great deal of embellishment because handworked detailing adds considerably to production costs. (For the purposes of this book, I'm defining embellishment as something which has been applied or added to the knitting, rather than a pattern designs such as Fair Isle or Intarsia, which are worked from charts as you knit.) Embellishment is the perfect way to express your interests, to reveal your personality, or to make a truly special gift for a friend. There is tremendous satisfaction to be gained from lavishing your care and attention on something you have made, and then to hear appreciative comments from friends and family.

Inspirations

If you find yourself lacking in inspiration, try taking a trip to a bookstore and look through the amazing variety of sewing and sewing-related magazines available. Even lifestyle magazines—filled with photographs of household furnishings embellished with tassels, cords, and buttons—can serve as inspiration. If you find yourself eager to embellish but always short on ideas, try keeping a clipping file of ideas that appeal to you, then staple it to an index card and jot down what you like about it or how you might use the idea in a sweater. Catalogs can also be a good source of inspiration. The people who assemble catalogs and magazines have had years of expensive and extensive art training from which you can benefit. Finally, remember to look around you. Observe! What is it, specifically, that appealed to you about the outfit you admired on a stranger this morning? Train yourself to notice details and learn to analyze them.

Limitations

There are some points to consider when choosing items to embellish garments. Of particular importance in knitwear is the weight of the embellishment. Will it simply be too heavy for the garment? Stretching and sagging are reliable signs that you need to choose something lighter. Even items as small as beads and buttons can vary greatly in weight from one type to another. Is the embellishment likely to snag the knitwear? If so, you may want to smooth out any rough edges with a metal jeweler's file. You also need to consider whether the embellishment is compatible with the type of cleaning the garment requires. Special-care embellishments may need to be detachable.

Sources

Embellishment items can be purchased from any number of mail-order and retail stores, but don't overlook thrift stores, garage sales, and flea markets. Here are a few of my favorite sources:

• Bead supply stores are a veritable Aladdin's cave of treasures. Spend a little time here and you will be amazed at what's available.

• Shops selling ethnic clothing and artifacts are good sources for shells, coins, and other possibilities. Such outlets frequently sell small jewelry items made with interesting bits and pieces like buttons and beads, carved bone and semiprecious stones that can be easily attached to knitwear.

• Dismantled jewelry, especially earrings, is another suitable embellishment source. A trip to a flea market will usually yield several wonderful bits and pieces of jewelry. There is no end to the styles and materials, and most pieces are lightweight enough to make them ideal for knitwear. Stabilize if necessary with a scrap of fabric at the back. Be careful not to overlook the jewelry findings themselves; those little clasps and closures often have interesting design elements and can be used decoratively on your knitwear or become a part of a special closure.

•And don't forget those magazines; the advertisers' index often leads to good mail-order suppliers.

Types of Embellishments

BEADS

There are a mind-boggling array of sizes and materials to choose from, ranging from the tiny and delicate to wonderfully dramatic ethnic pieces. Sew the beads on in decorative patterns, randomly, or in conjunction with other embellishments.

BUTTONS

Quite literally whole books have been written on the subject and there are several ideas scattered throughout this book which you may use on any garment. (See pages 37, 88, and 99 for a few examples.) Here are a few of my favorite ways to use buttons:

- Group buttons in themes, e.g. for a cat lover use a variety of different cat buttons.

- No law says a button should function only as a closure; try placing just one stunning vintage button high on the shoulder or on one side of a collar.

- Use groups of buttons on cuffs, collars, pockets, or around hem bands.

- Place buttons on top of buttons, varying their colors and shapes.

- Sew buttons on through patches of ultrasuede. Think about cutting this in decorative shapes such as a fish or a star.

- Make a feature of one fuctional button by sewing others decoratively around it.

- Next time you're shopping for buttons, consider that many come in graduated sizes, offering you various design opportunities.

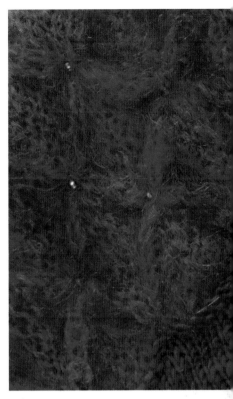

Small beads sewn onto knitting

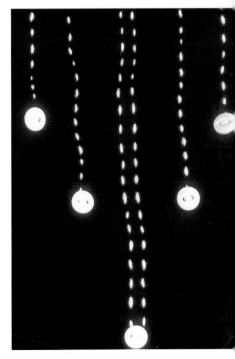

Running stitch and button embellishment

119

Button and bobble
embellishment

CORDS AND RIBBONS

Most types of cord and ribbon are very decorative on knitwear and can work well as fasteners. In addition to the lush varieties sold in fabric and bead shops, also look for cords and ribbons in drapery departments and on old handbags and coats in thrift shops. Cords and ribbons usually thread easily through knitted stitches, making it simple to achieve regular patterns by counting the stitches/rows. Other options include couching the cording down on the knitting or threading it through beads before attaching.

KNITTED BOBBLES

These are among my favorite embellishments. You may make and attach them separately (see instructions on page 000) or you can pick up a stitch on the garment at the desired spot and knit on the bobble. Bobbles can be attached randomly or in patterns. They can be large and exuberant or small and delicate.

A fun option is to secure a large, plain button in place with a bobble. Simply thread the bobble yarn ends through the holes in the button, then through the sweater, and tie off on the back side.

KNITTED FLAPS

These may be points, squares, or rectangles. There are two basic ways of knitting flaps. To make one, first knit the flap in the desired shape and size. Bind off the stitches and then attach it with a button or hand stitching.

A second way of making flaps is to pick up the required number of stitches at the point you want to place your flap and knit about an inch (2.5 cm). Knit 2 tog at each side on every row until one stitch remains, then draw the yarn tightly through. Now you can further embellish your flaps with embroidery or with dangling beads.

Knitted flap embellishments

Leather pieces also make attractive flaps. It can be cut in a variety of shapes and used in many ways. (Consider ultrasuede as a leather substitute if you don't want your sweater to require dry cleaning.) Leather supply shops often sell goody bags filled with small scrap pieces, as do many mail-order companies.

CROCHET

Decorative edgings can be created on knitwear with basic crochet stitches. Crocheted chain of novelty threads can be used in a variety of ways to embellish a garment.

EMBROIDERY

Those of you who are accomplished in this area will have your own favorite stitches and techniques, but even beginners can create great effects with just a few colorful stitches. Find a basic embroidery book with good illustrations of the running stitch, the chain stitch, the stem stitch, and French knots. Another option is to thread a needle with a contrasting color of yarn and add decorative designs by weaving the yarn through the knitting.

POMPONS

Pompons are very effective when you think small—make tiny ones in variegated or multicolored yarns. A plain black evening sweater can be embellished most effectively in this manner. You can make these in the time-honored kids' tradition, using circles of cardboard, but today some nifty little pompon makers are readily available through yarn stores and mail-order catalogs.

TASSELS

Many good books on this subject are available. An obvious place for tassels is at the bottom of a garment, but why should this limit you? Make them from cotton or silk embroidery flosses and attach them where you might least expect them, such as in rows around a sleeve, at the shoulder seams, or decorating the front bands of a jacket. Big and bold tassels can be made with a few leather strands incorporated in the yarn and then secured with a dramatic bead. For an elegant look, try threading dainty glass beads through the yarns in tiny tassels.

Crochet embellishment

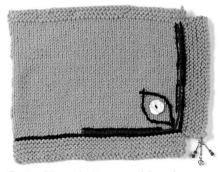

Embroidery, button, and bead embellishment

Running stitch embellishment

FRINGE

Fringe is a versatile embellishment option. Consider adding fringe to the edges of a collar, pockets, or just above the cuff on a sleeve. Fringe can also be stitched on vertically from the front hem band up and over the shoulder.

APPLIQUÉS

A variety of appliqués are available at fabric stores. Try scattering the little ribbon roses you can buy by the yard or in packages from the fabric shops on a plain sweater to create a dainty look, particularly if the sweater is in a soft yarn. For evening, a few tiny mother-of-pearl buttons or small beads can further enhance this embellishment.

PATCHES

Use nonfraying material such as leather, ultrasuede, or felt to create custom patches. Sew on with bold stitches and embellish further with buttons if desired. For a great "poor boy" look, make patches from cloth and leave the raw edges unfinished.

METHODS OF APPLICATION

Stabilizers—interfacing, muslin scraps, waste canvas, bridal tulle, or other commercial products—can be used behind the knitting to make application easier. When possible, make your embellishments removable. Buttons, for example, are easily attached with cords and pearl thread. If you are using a larger embellishment, consider applying it with Velcro or a snap: just sew one section of the Velcro or snap to the embellishment and the other in place on the garment. Making embellishments removable simplifies cleaning of the garment and gives you the freedom to change your mind in the future.

Appliqué embellishment

Rather than discard a damaged sweater you are fond of, consider some embellishment to cover the hole or stain. Nonknitting friends come shrieking to me with their favorite damaged sweaters on a regular basis. One particularly distraught college student was thrilled to bits when I stitched up the evidence of her puppy's teething and added small beaded flaps to cover the sewing repairs. The sweater shown here was embellished with padded appliqués and embroidery.

Acknowledgments

First and foremost I thank my husband, Ron, for his loving support which made the project possible. I am grateful to Carol Taylor, Lark's publishing director, who had the original idea and invited me to write this book. Considerable thanks are due to my editor, Dawn Cusick, whose good humor and amazing organizational skills kept me on track far more than she realizes.

Sally Poole helped and encouraged me a great deal with the knitting. Jane Lippmann cheered me along with enthusiasm from start to finish.

I also greatly appreciate the creative team at Lark: Susan McBride for her wonderful design work on this book, Evan Bracken for his fabulous photography, Dana Irwin for her joyous contributions, and Hannes Charen, Tom Metcalf, and Kathy Holmes for all their hard work.

Thanks are also due to the people who generously donated their time to model the sweaters and their homes for location photography: April Carder and Scott Corely for the use of their barn, flock of sheep, and kitchen for lunch; Sarah Boelt for horse help; Amanda Cone for use of her barn and grounds; Jacque Stevens for the use of her lovely home and grounds; models Davida and Meredith Falk; and child models Arden and Baily Cone, Henry Bravo, Faye Stevens, and Margaret Rose Murphy.

Finally, I would like to thank the following companies who shared samples of their yarns for the sweaters: Anny Blatt, Berroco, Inc., Brown Sheep Co., Inc., Cascade Yarns, Inc., Classic Elite, Ironstone Yarns, Muench Yarns, Plymouth Yarn Co., Tahki Imports, Ltd., Westminster Fibers (distributor of Rowan), Skacel Collection, Inc. (distributor of Zitron), Trendsetter Yarns, Filatura di Crosa, Missoni & The Stacy Charles Collection, Prism Yarns, Colinette Yarns Unique Kolors, Ltd., Lane Borgosesia, Mountain Colors, Cotton Clouds, and Joslyns Fiber Farm.

Bibliography

Barnes, Mary Galpin, ed. *Knitting Tips & Trade Secrets.* Newtown, Connecticut: Taunton Press, 1996.

Buss, Katharina. *Big Book of Knitting.* New York: Sterling Publishing, 1996.

Epstein, Nicki. *Knitted Embellishments.* Loveland, Colorado: Interweave Press,1999.

Hiatt, June Hemmons. *The Principles of Knitting.* New York: Simon and Schuster, 1988.

Square, Vicki. The Knitters Companion. Loveland, Colorado: Interweave Press, 1996.

Morrell, Anne. *The Techniques of Indian Embroidery.* Loveland: Interweave Press, 1995.

Stanley, Montse. *Knitters Handbook.* Pleasantville: Readers Digest Association, 1993.

Vogue Knitting, eds. Vogue Knitting: *The Ultimate Knitting Book.* New York: Pantheon Books, 1989.

Zimmerman, Elizabeth. *Knitting Without Tears.* New York: Charles Scribners Sons, 1971.

Index